THE POWER
TO GOVERN

Da Capo Press Reprints in

AMERICAN CONSTITUTIONAL AND LEGAL HISTORY

GENERAL EDITOR: LEONARD W. LEVY

Claremont Graduate School

THE POWER
TO GOVERN

The Constitution—Then and Now

---

by

WALTON H. HAMILTON
and DOUGLASS ADAIR

DA CAPO PRESS • NEW YORK • 1972

Library of Congress Cataloging in Publication Data

Hamilton, Walton Hale, 1881-1958.
    The power to govern.
    (Da Capo Press reprints in American constitutional
and legal history)
    Includes bibliographical references.
    1. U.S. Constitution. 2. U.S.—Constitutional
history. 3. U.S.—Politics and government.
I. Adair, Douglass, joint author. II. Title.
JK271.H43   1972   342'.73'029   77-37759
ISBN 0-306-70433-1

Published by Da Capo Press, Inc.
A Subsidiary of Plenum Publishing Corporation
227 West 17th Street, New York, N.Y. 10011

THE POWER
TO GOVERN

The Constitution—Then and Now

---

by

WALTON H. HAMILTON
and DOUGLASS ADAIR

W. W. NORTON & COMPANY, INC.
Publishers   *New York*

PRINTED IN THE UNITED STATES OF AMERICA

FOR THE PUBLISHERS BY QUINN & BODEN COMPANY, INC.

To

JOHN GILBERT WINANT

is inscribed this brief account of

THE CHARACTER, PARTICULARS, AND
DOMAIN OF COMMERCE
the Regulation of which
was Entrusted to the Congress of the United States,

by

THE CONSTITUTION OF 1787,

as it appears in

The Language of the People, the Prevailing Climate of
Opinion, the Economy of the Time, the Problems Current to the Nation, the DEBATES
in the CONVENTION, and the
DOCUMENT ITSELF;

together with

Some Mention of the Specific Powers over War, Treaties, Tariffs, Taxes and Excises, and the other Devices
through which
such an Authority was to be Exercised.

Contents

· I ·

The Appeal from Gloss to Text

A FATE of a public policy hangs on the validity of an act; an act awaits the judgment in a case; a case turns upon the boundaries of a word. This is the way of the law. The caption of Carter v. Carter Coal Co.—save for the suspicion aroused by its patronymic beat—smacks in no way of the unusual. It is technically the first of a quartet of kindred suits which are Nos. 636, 649, 650, and 651, in the calendar of the United States Supreme Court for the October term of 1935. In reality it marks the most important judicial battle of recent years over the power of the Federal Government in the control of industry. The resulting decree has—for the time at least —placed bituminous coal outside the realm of national regulation; and the result was reached because the majority of the justices could not make the word "commerce" in the Constitution comprehend all that was included in the challenged statute.

A decision in a novel case achieved by a bare majority can hardly be called decisive. Nor can it be asserted beyond a reasonable doubt that the exploration of the frontiers of the term "commerce" by the learned spokesman for the Court has been exhaustive. It is not impossible, with precedents from the Court's records, to contrive a plausible argument against the recent judgment. And, outside of vaulted chambers and the law reports, there is a none-too-orderly world of affairs that will do its part to keep the issue alive. As no other cause of late, the Carter case lifted a little the veil of legalism, raised sharply the question of federal authority, and brought into the open the role of the judiciary in the public control of business.

Yet, for all its drama, the Carter case did not appear unheralded. An enduring struggle has been going on for decades between the political state and the economic order.[1] For decades an industrial order blundered its tumultuous way into being; the market, the machine, and the corporation, instruments of its coming, were strange to the people; and its growth eluded the established ways of regulation. But as soon as the outline of the newer economic order stood out in relief and its shortcomings came to be appreciated, the state began to subdue it to the common good. In a series of statutes it attempted to preserve competition, to establish minimum labor standards, to protect the consumer, to insure to

[1] Footnote references will be found on page 195 ff.

business rivals a fair field, to regulate public utilities, and to subordinate money-making to the general welfare. As the legislature responded to demands for control, the interests which found such statutes distasteful appealed to the judiciary, invoked the sanctions of the Constitution, and attempted to protect the frontiers of "industry " [2] against government interference.

The struggle of business against state runs on. Its shifting result has been affected by circumstance and expediency, the rhythm of reform and relapse, and the alternation of good times and bad. As the "great depression of 1929" appeared to invite entries in red, hasten bankruptcies, and create unemployment, the opposition for the moment crumbled; and the national government was besought by business to extend its control over a demoralized domain of private enterprise. As industry felt "the recovery" it renewed its challenge, and Acts of Congress had again to undergo the constitutional scrutiny of the courts.

It was not until the depression had passed its peak that suits involving the New Deal reached the Supreme Court. At the beginning of 1935 the doctrine of the delegation of power—which had long lain almost dormant—was employed to express disapproval of the federal control of oil.[3] A little later the action of the government in the manipulation of the currency—popularly known as "going off the gold standard"—received the approval, or at least did not provoke the veto, of the

Court.[4] A year later and by a single vote the Court struck down a railway retirement act [5] on the ground that its subject matter lay outside the province of interstate commerce. And hard upon its heels came the holding in the Schechter case that the slaughtering of poultry neither was nor directly concerned commerce among the several states.[6]

In the October term of 1935 the series of New Deal cases was continued. An attempt to accommodate an expanded agricultural system to the loss of its foreign market, by the use of such devices as a processing tax and a bonus for restriction of acreage, was held to be an unwarranted exercise of federal authority.[7] A number of tangled issues emerged in a suit which challenged the legality of the Tennessee Valley Authority.[8] A majority of the Court were evidently of the opinion that the Federal Government had no general constitutional power to generate and sell electrical energy. But some members were not disturbed by such doubts, and others persuaded themselves that the production of the electric current was a mere incident to the exercise of the powers over navigation and war. So between the two groups votes were available to sanction within severe limits this particular incursion of the government into private enterprise.[9]

At this strategic moment appeared the Carter case.[10] The plight of the bituminous coal industry has been notorious, and its regulation little short of a national necessity. An excess of productive capacity brings in its wake an intense struggle for orders, want of satisfactory working conditions, a wage too low to support a decent living, and a plague of bankruptcies. The market—for all the repute of the law of supply and demand—is unable to bring order into the affairs of the industry. The coal-producing states, as they testified in briefs presented to the Supreme Court, have found the problem beyond their competence. The sole choice is between action by the Federal Government and industrial chaos. Upon this point the parties to the industry and students of the subject are unanimous. After repeated investigation by special commissions, and a consideration of the subject which ran through years, Congress passed the Guffey Coal Act.[11] It set up a coal commission, brought capacity and production under control, and provided for an authoritative determination of wages and of prices.[12]

Although generally acceptable to operators and mine workers the act was challenged by a minority of the industry in the name of the higher law. A suit in the District of Columbia [13] won a qualified, and one in Kentucky a complete, victory for the government; [14] and, with all dispatch, the causes were appealed. The Supreme Court made no attempt to controvert the facts or to challenge the plight of the industry.[15] The sole question raised by the majority was the authority of Congress to pass the act.[16] The sanction must, in the opinion of the Court, derive from the commerce clause or be entirely lacking and the power over "commerce among the several states" did not extend to the regulation of wages and working conditions. The price-fixing conditions, despite a declaration in the statute to the contrary, were held not severable; [17] and hence they, too, had to fall. As for the impost on tonnage, it was not a tax but a penalty, and was likewise null and void. And as for the validity of the price-fixing provisions, had they by Congress been embodied in a statute all to themselves, that was a hypothetical inquiry. And to a question so devoid of concretions, the Court would give no answer.[18]

It is unnecessary to quarrel with the Court over the exact constitutional questions which the case presents. It is enough that the matter of getting an unruly economic order under control breaks squarely upon the power of the Federal Government over "commerce among the several states." In the word "commerce" the whole issue lies. In the meanings with which it will come to be endowed by the Court, the conflict will eventually be resolved.

The word "commerce" has no natural boundaries. In ordinary speech and business usage no rule of certainty tells where commerce leaves off and something else begins. Nor has the Court always been able to sever the tentacles which bind its activities to the economic order and to erect in commerce a lordly domain apart. At other times it has recognized an intimate—even an indi-visible—relationship between the production of certain commodities and their sale in a national market. In sustaining an Act of Congress imposing a scheme of regulation upon stock-yards and meat-packers it has linked production with distribution in a "stream of commerce." [19] Its decision, in sustaining an act designed to curb the excesses of trading in grain futures, recognizes that commerce reaches far beyond the market-place.[20] It has, in the name of commerce, allowed the anti-trust acts to be applied to the internal affairs, even the labor relations, of manufacturing concerns.[21] And, in respect to bituminous coal, it has given recognition to the unity and continuity of the process of mining and market-ing.[22]

But on this occasion the word was pent within severe verbal limits. According to Mr. Justice Sutherland, the word commerce "as used in the Constitution" means "intercourse for the purposes of trade." [23] In broad terms it "includes" transportation, purchase, sale, and exchange of commodities between the citizens of the different states. But the domain of the word must begin with the interstate movement of the goods; it cannot reach back to comprehend "the employment of men, the fixing of their wages, hours of labor, and working conditions," [24] or the activities which result in the extraction of coal from the mine. All such conditions, circumstances, and operations, antecedent as they may be to interstate

traffic, constitute "production" and are "local in character." The federal power is to be exercised over commodities in movement; it is not to be applied before
they commence their interstate journeys or have "come
to rest "[25] within a state's territory. Thus "commerce"
is given the quality of mobility; a clean-cut line is set
about its domain; and all that relates to "production" is
denied benefit of its verbal coverage.

The idea of the insulation of commerce from the
impinging world of industry did not emerge for the
first time in the Carter case. Mr. Justice Sutherland can
cite numerous holdings and innumerable dicta to his
purpose. He finds the distinction sharply expressed in a
case which goes back almost half a century, in which
a state act prohibiting the manufacture of alcoholic
beverages was upheld even though the whole of the
product went into interstate commerce.[26] A little later,
in an opinion which allowed "the sugar trust" to escape
the tentacles of the anti-trust law, it is stated that
"commerce succeeds to manufacture, and is not a part
of it."[27] A few years later the Court explicitly declared
that mining "like manufacturing is a local business," the
character of which persists even though conducted in
close connection with interstate commerce.[28]

In the famous Schechter case,[29] the Court found the
focus of commerce in the movement of goods and made
the disturbance of the interstate stream the criterion of
federal control. And a few years ago the current bench,

with Mr. Justice Sutherland as its spokesman, had found that there is "in judicial contemplation" a pause between the generation and the transmission of electricity.[30] A veritable array of cases attests the variety of purposes for which commerce has been erected into a separate domain. It is not without the authority of his own Court [31] that Mr. Justice Sutherland concludes that the production and manufacture of a commodity, and its sale and transportation, are "two distinct and separate activities." [32]

The decision of the Court is more than a judgment in an important case. It involves more than the power of Congress to prescribe a way of order for bituminous coal; the plight of textiles, of boots and shoes, and of lumber is equally notorious; and the factors which bring disorder into the affairs of many another industry are nation-wide in their scope. A growing opinion has it that competition is inadequate to its economic task; that the matter lies beyond the competence of the several states; and that the real choice is between federal regulation and industrial disorder. Moreover, the judicial scrutiny which can draw narrow lines about commerce, can discover severities in "due process of law," [33] bring an improper delegation of powers to its judgment, and perhaps even draw from between the lines of the Constitution rigid standards for legislation which were never tucked away there. The formal bother is over the frontiers of commerce; the real issue is the power of the government to govern.

There is nothing unseemly in matters of public policy turning upon niceties of diction. Here a great issue waits upon an ordeal of words and invites an excursion into English, judicial, and economic usage. The Constitution is at once a document, a code of judge-made law, and a changing body of understandings. It may be that the document compels such an interpretation, as those who bless their opinions with the sanctions of venerable words would have us believe. It may be that changing occasions in the life of a people bring fresh meanings to abiding words and make ancient verbal symbols instruments of their purpose. Or it may be that "the gloss, not the text, is the thing," as an old Simeon proverb has it. But whatever the Constitution and the way of the mind with it, we are by judicial usage compelled to look at the words in the light of the utterances of the founders. If we are to probe the meaning of its clauses, we must call as a witness the age that produced it.

An utterance of the Court is the law; a quotation of a quotation has double authority. A statement by Mr. Justice Lamar is approvingly cited by Mr. Justice Sutherland, "No distinction is more popular to the common mind, or more clearly expressed in economic and political literature than that between manufacture and commerce." Set down this statement, make it a text, and add a question-mark. There emerges an issue of the dependence of a great public policy upon a simple verbal usage.

~~~~~~

· II ·

The Crisis of Seventeen Eighty-Seven

---

1. *The Breach in the Economy*

A CENTURY-and-a-half has elapsed since the event. It is
hardly to be expected that we can now recapture with
complete accuracy the character, particulars, and domain of the "commerce among the several states" the
regulation of which was entrusted to the Congress by
the Fathers in 1787. None of them left a canonical
statement of what might come to be comprehended
within a few simple words. An attempt to surprise their
import by interpretation, piecing together bits of evidence, and arguing from contemporary circumstance is
not without its hazards. An extraction of meaning from
the conditions of the times, the exigencies to be met,
and the disposition of the delegates yields something less
than absolute truth. But to disregard available evidence
is to ignore the events which called "the supreme law
of the land" into being and to allow its provisions un-

critically to be endowed with a meaning from today. Its character was—it had to be—shaped within the general circumstances which called it forth.

Words are the names of things. The "commerce" of the great document is not a legalistic category to be explored in the law reports, but the miscellany of economic activities which were everyday realities to the men of 1787. The genesis of the Constitution lies in the controversies between the independent states and the difficulties which "interests" had experienced under the Articles of Confederation. Into this world of affairs which they knew, it is not easy for us to enter. We look back from the vantage point of an economic order transformed by a continuous cultural revolution; and it requires a heroic act of reconstruction to free our clouded vision from all that the intervening decades have brought.

In 1787 the household—an all but self-sufficient economic world in miniature—was the unit of production. Various activities in house, pasture, field, and woodland provided the family with its living. A division of labor as a rule assigned the heavy work to the men, the housework to the women, and the chores to the children. It was, for the great mass of the people, a landed and all but moneyless economy. Almost all the processing of foods and of raw materials was done by the original producer. The farmer killed his own cattle and hogs; smoked, pickled, or dried his own beef, hams, and fish.

He ground his own grain into meal or flour, or for a toll had the task performed at the neighborhood mill. The domestic economy provided its own fats, candles, hides, shoes, and clothing. The washing was done on the place with homemade soap or lye; the tanning, with bark or berry brew. Textiles of the warmer sort were spun and woven from wool, flax, or cotton fiber. The forests provided fuel and crude furniture; dishes, bowls, platters, rakes, brooms, baskets and farm tools were fashioned by hand from wood. The family domain—through gun, plow, barnyard, and smoke-house—provided almost all of a family's necessities. The living was won, far away from commerce, by family arts not yet in want of regulation.

But the economy of the household had its nexus with the world beyond. The crafts had been brought over from the old countries; and in the towns the cobbler, the weaver, and the blacksmith for a consideration plied their common—or commercial—callings. The tradesman received materials from his customer and fashioned them into custom-made articles; when he was not busy upon orders he produced ready-made goods to be peddled, sold to the neighborhood storekeeper, or exchanged for the wherewithal of a living.

A number of arts had become detached from the domestic economy, and were on the way toward becoming "industries" in the next century. In cities like Philadelphia, Wilmington, and Baltimore there were "com-

mercial" flour mills; around Cape Fear and along the
Mohawk River, commercial sawmills; and in New Jersey, Pennsylvania, and Virginia, commercial furnaces
wherein iron was wrought. Some trades had outgrown
their domestic habitat and their products had come to
be nationally known. The shoes of Lynn, cloth of
Providence, the stockings knit at Germantown, and the
tinware of Berlin, Connecticut, were all famous "mar-
ket-goods." They were manufactured on the putting-
out system; they were not, like local wares, "bespoken"
or "store" goods. Thus a fringe of commerce had come
to skirt the realm of petty agrarian autonomies.

The national economy rested squarely upon agriculture. A good nine-tenths of the people depended solely
upon it for existence. The forest, the sea, and the streams
invited trapping, lumbering, and fishing. The production of tar, resin and potash provided supplementary
occupations. The skilled arts were appendages to the
farms; and as a means of additional income many of the
artisans worked up their own products. A stream of
manufactured articles from overseas added variety to a
standard of living resting upon the products of the soil.

But the advantages of commerce did not go unappre-
ciated. The ordinary person might be content with the
simple necessities yielded by farm and frontier. But if
families of substance and standing were to enjoy the
comforts and amenities of life, they had to look to foreign trade for the wares of London and the goods of

the Orient. A demand from overseas exacted its recompense. It drew tobacco from Virginia, rice and indigo from South Carolina, ships from New England, and created cities like Boston, Philadelphia, New York, Baltimore, and Charleston to command the arteries of trade. At the beginning of the Revolution at least two-thirds of this commerce had been with England and its colonies. Tobacco and other staples reached foreign countries by way of London. An extensive intercourse had sprung up with the "sugar islands" of the British West Indies. The planters of Barbados and St. Kitts were dependent upon the northern colonies for food supplies, finished lumber, and draft animals for field or mill. The raw sugar and molasses which they sent in return created the refineries of Boston, New York, and Philadelphia, and got the rum distilleries of New England off to a lusty start. Rum in its turn supplied our Revolutionary forefathers with their favorite drink, served as a lubricant of barter with the Indians, and provided a *quid pro quo* in the African slave trade. A favorable trade with the West Indies left its balance in specie—cash in hand to the colonial merchant to carry on his trafficking and serve as capital for further expansion. London and the West Indies were vital points in a national system which comprehended America.

Commerce thus performed a national office. It offered markets abroad, created a territorial division of labor, allowed material resources to be fully exploited, brought in luxury wares and habits touched by taste, and raised the stately houses of the great families. Commerce promoted intercourse, drew households together into a community, supplied the communication necessary to the creation of a culture, and provided the tissue of activities essential to the existence of a vital government. And commerce gave to the thirteen colonies a distinctive place in the planned economy of imperial England.

In like manner the men of commerce played a national role in the events leading up to the Revolution; their changing attitude toward Britain from 1763 until 1776 is an accurate barometer of the progress of the rebellion.[1] Merchants and moneyed men were from their very dealings the most immediate links between the sections of British America. The commercial interest, comprised a distinct merchant class in the northern and middle colonies in close contact with the planters of the South. The latter, as shippers of their own staples, were merchants of a glorified sort. It was the only integrated group in colonial society that transcended state and geographical divisions. As a bloc it had already developed a consciousness of identity of interest. The merchants, therefore, played a unique part in the fusion of the scattered complaints of the separate colonies and their direction into a unified movement of protest against the mother country. As conservatives they did not countenance the drastic program advocated by extremists of the Samuel Adams cast. It was the trading interest that acted as a moderating force in 1765 once the Stamp Act was repealed. It was the trading interest that in 1770 lessened the tension raised by the quickly modified Townshend duties. It was only when the Tea Act of 1773 forced most of the commercial class into active opposition or interested neutrality, that the way was cleared for the radicals. The interests of commerce were thereafter directed mainly toward solidifying the colonies for revolt. The appeal to arms followed shortly.

The significance of the separation from Great Britain can hardly be exaggerated. It had its political, economic and social consequences; in every aspect of culture it presented serious problems of adjustment. In the imperial system there had arisen a cultural as well as economic division of labor. In medicine, law, literature, education, science, and the fine arts the colonials had looked to England for leadership and training. The Revolution threw English prestige into eclipse and cut off the maturing influence of a more established society. The character of the struggle, with its cries of "Independence" and "Freedom," stimulated a national consciousness which carried an indigenous Americanism into all fields of national endeavor. The frontier came to replace the metropolis as the dominant influence in a developing civilization. America was quite unable to supply the discipline essential to distinction in the intellectual pursuits. The expulsion of the Tories—whose ranks included "the rich and well-born"—was a further blow to the learned professions. As a result a national lapse occurred from the intellectual standards of the later Eighteenth Century. The immediate effect of a separation, essential as it was to a distinctive American culture, was an initial period of isolation and inhibition in respect to intellectual pursuits. It required many years to establish the relationships essential to new cultural growth. Separation too entailed readjustments for the commerce of the new republic. The event of independence came as a shock to the whole economy of Great Britain.

At the surrender of Cornwallis in 1783, the commercial interests of the colonies had every reason to be optimistic about the prospect ahead. An economy geared to a self-sufficient agrarian population could suffer no dearth of "the articles of commerce," even after eight years of war. There was on hand in America a relatively large supply of hard money—"the medium of commerce"; for the large sums of specie sent out to provision and pay the discomfited British forces had finally come to rest in the coffers of honest patriot traders. There was an energetic revival of foreign trade; merchants bought goods abroad freely on credit to supply a market greedy after years of deprivation for the "luxuries and conveniences" that only Europe could supply. Scores of home industries, established during the commercial blockade, expanded with like confidence. All in all the mercantile classes were optimistic and eager to try out their new-won freedom and to act their part in the world's "theater of commerce."

But the rosy dream of commercial prosperity that bedazzled men in 1783 was soon exploded. Infant industries discovered that they could not compete with the foreign manufactures that poured in through the eastern ports. Importations speedily siphoned a large part of the ready specie from the country and by 1785 a real stringency had developed.[2] Independence made it difficult to recoup this loss of precious metal by foreign exchange. The preference accorded colonial products in the English market was lost; the bounties which had promoted productions, such as the naval stores of North Carolina, were withdrawn; and the ships of New England were deprived of a share in the lucrative carrying trade between London and points abroad. A major disaster was the closing of the British West Indies to American vessels. This trade, which in 1770 had employed five hundred vessels and disposed of $3,500,000 worth of exports, was threatened with legal extinction; and, if it could not be held, there was little chance of finding a substitute market elsewhere. But the old channels of trade were too deeply grooved to be disregarded. The planters of the British West Indies were dependent upon the northern states for food supplies; and the trade was so profitable to the Americans that a British decree was not enough to abolish it. With the connivance of local British officials, smuggling, trans-shipment of goods from the neighboring Danish, Dutch, and French islands, and other flagrant illegalities flourished. Yet a system beset with such an array of cost, annoyance, indirection, and complication could not replace the old relationship. For a century the "advancement of national commerce and manufactures" had been "a point of state policy in all the councils of Europe."[8] The exports of the independent and united States were now confronted by the hostile mercantile systems of England, France, Spain, Portugal, and Holland.

Independence also made it difficult to find a vent for the surplus produce of American agriculture. Great Britain, alive to the advantages accruing from the disorganization of the thirteen states, refused to conclude with Congress a treaty of commerce. Instead it regulated its intercourse with America by Orders in Council. France had been a comrade-in-arms during the Revolution, and Spain was a neighbor who owned all the trans-Mississippi area and most of South America; yet neither would make any mercantile concessions to the infant republic. Alliances with foreign nations, essential to make the commerce of America a part of a larger commercial system, were wanting; and the authority to contrive a continental economy for America lay in the hands of independent states. The action taken by the thirteen separate sovereignties in 1785-1786 only deepened the gloom that hung over the commercial outlook.

Moreover, independence had brought in its train great changes in the personnel of the state legislatures. The call to arms, the excitement of the crisis, the rationalization of a cause threw into sharp relief political and social abuses of long standing. As the authority of the Crown had weakened, the balance of power had shifted rapidly. The Tories had gone over to the enemy, emigrated to Canada, or lapsed into a quiescent minority; and among the patriots the radicals came into power. The way was clear for swift and drastic changes in the social structure; and the legislatures, controlled by the popular party, put into effect a series of far-reaching reforms abridging the perquisites of property, curbing the powers of the church, widening the base of suffrage, and enlarging the rights of the underprivileged. A social revolution attended the progress of arms; and, when peace came, the more democratical element—agrarian and not commercial in its outlook—was well entrenched within the law-making bodies of the several states.[4]

The cause of the debtor was in the ascendancy. The relief of his distress was an object of general legislative solicitude. Acts emanating from state capitals made it easy for debtors to postpone or evade obligations of contract which they had voluntarily assumed.[5] The "stay laws" of Virginia and South Carolina, allowing the payment of debt in installments, amounted to virtual moratoria. The courts of North Carolina were closed to actions for debt. The older restrictions upon the dishonest acts of bankruptcy were relaxed and confused. In the "Pine Barren Act," South Carolina conferred the attributes of money upon various sorts of property. Any kind of land was made legal tender at two-thirds of its value as determined by three independent arbiters. It was therefore easy for the canny individual to offer lands situated so far away that the cost of appraisal would swallow up the debt, and usually creditors preferred a surrender of their claims to the wanton indulgence of throwing good money after bad. In like manner the sincere tender to Charleston merchants of stocks of grain, fodder, or tobacco assembled some two hundred miles inland was a polite form of repudiation.

But the expedient most popular to the legislatures was a cheaper legal tender; and in a number of commonwealths the printing presses busily responded with quantities of paper money. The proficiency of Rhode Island in this pecuniary competition won universal and lasting renown. Such statutory indulgences played hob with established values and threw into disorder the system of prices. These issues of paper money aroused the commercial classes and brought genuine distress to creditors.[6] But even where sound money commanded legislative respect, trouble was not to be avoided. New England, Rhode Island alone dissenting, stood adamant

against paper emissions. It was the one section, however, in which actual violence broke out. Shays' rebellion in Massachusetts, although quickly put down by
the state militia,[7] was a tocsin sounding the alarm to all
men of property in all the states. Acts for the relief of
debtors became instruments in the game of politics and
provoked "warfare and retaliation among the states." [8]

The spirit of competitive localism found expression in
the imposition of taxes and the regulation of trade. At
the close of the Revolution all the states, save New
Jersey, imposed small duties on imports to raise revenue.
As the burden of war debts was felt and the urge to
protect domestic products grew insistent, the system
was extended and the rates were raised. In New England and most of the Middle States almost all wares
were subject to ever-increasing rates. As a result an
angry quarrel between New York and her neighbors,
Connecticut and New Jersey, almost broke into armed
strife; into this feud Massachusetts and New Hampshire were drawn by the attempt of Connecticut to re-
taliate against neighboring states and trade directly with
England. Controversies only slightly less violent engaged the other states. South Carolina bickered with
Georgia. North Carolina complained that South Carolina and Virginia taxed its consumption; Virginia, in
turn, protested that Maryland and Pennsylvania laid a
"tribute" on its commodities at the ports of Baltimore
and Philadelphia. The complaint was general that the

maritime states were regulating their important ports to the disadvantage of their non-maritime neighbors.

Independence was an accomplished fact; yet its translation into the structure of the national economy was lagging. As yet foreign trade had not found its revised pattern; nor had the affairs of the several states been quickened into going concerns. An integration of economic activities into an orderly system is no easy task. As an aspect of a novel venture into nationalism it was doubly difficult; and from the Treaty of Peace in 1783 to the Call to Convention in 1787 little headway was made. Amid the confusion of the times, the problem of accommodation to independence had been stated with increasing emphasis especially by the commercial class. For traders could see the deplorable effects of the current situation in their ledgers and sense the pressing need of counteracting the trends toward disunion. The animosities attending the control of commerce by multiple agencies might easily shatter the shaky Confederation into warring entities. It seemed high time to call a halt to an amateur fling at nationalism on the part of each of thirteen separate commonwealths.

2. *The Moves Towards Repair*

All of this provoked appropriate reactions from the people. To the great mass of the population, living in the domestic economy, it was a matter of small account.

Buttressed behind the barriers of an agricultural self-sufficiency, they were little affected by the general trends in trade. A few luxuries might be lost; there might be pinching in the use of tea or sugar; but livings could still be wrested from the soil. To the commercial economy of town, merchant, and staple crop, however, it was quite another matter. A hazard to the intricate network of trade was a threat to livelihood and opportunity. Although the mercantile group was a mere fragment of the people, its importance was out of all proportion to its numbers.

To the moneyed interest a move towards a greater unity and a more studied direction of commerce was imperative. It came as a concerted demand from every state in the Confederation from Massachusetts to Georgia; for "committees of correspondence" had welded the local groups into a national bloc intent upon reform.[9] Even before the Revolution was won, delegates in Congress were recommending to the states that it was "indispensably necessary"—if enactments "partial or contrary to common interest" were to be avoided—to vest the "superintending of commercial regulations of every state" in the national legislature.[10] Again in 1784, it was urged upon the states that powers be vested in Congress to pass a navigation act and to prohibit for a period of fifteen years imports from any nation that would not make treaties of commerce with the Union. Great Britain's "destructive" system and her regulations [11] of the West Indian trade are noted specifically. But like the previous proposal it came to naught. The state legislatures showed no disposition to surrender so integral an attribute of sovereignty as the regulation of commerce.

In the following year, 1785, a national regulation of commerce invited a move of a different character. In the Virginia Assembly, James Madison proposed that Virginia as a state take the initiative in suggesting to the other states that Congress be authorized to regulate trade. The merchants and business men of Philadelphia petitioned the legislature of Pennsylvania to the same effect. Congress, they felt, should have "a full and entire power over the commerce of the United States" and they assured the legislature that "there was a disposition in the mercantile interest of Pennsylvania favorable thereto." [12]

As 1785 drew to a close no further action had been taken. Virginia again took a new tack and proposed that the states send commissioners to examine "the trade of the United States . . . and of the said states"; and to discuss "how far a uniform system in their commercial regulations may be necessary to their common interests and permanent harmony." [13] The meeting was called for September of 1786 in Annapolis, in the State of Maryland. But by the time the commissioners met, scores of substantial citizens had come to the conclusion that vesting control of commerce in the Congress of the

Confederation would be futile or downright dangerous. The urgency of commercial and fiscal questions required that broad powers of correction should be entrusted only to a government "so braced, changed or altered" as to be able to wield them.

For during the summer of 1786 the repute of the existing government reached a new low. It seemed obvious that the effort to prop up the flimsy fabric of Confederation credit by the national duty on imports was doomed to failure.[14] As a consequence federal paper was selling at from one-sixth to one-twentieth of par value. The violent insurrection of that "desperate debtor," Daniel Shays, had flamed during the summer in Massachusetts. Rhode Island, that "nest of vipers, mixed with adders foul," was still solving all problems by fresh issues of worthless paper. And the several commonwealths continued to fortify their frontiers against the commercial invasion of their neighbors. It was, under the circumstances, a foregone conclusion that whatever forward-reaching proposals might emerge from the Annapolis Convention would meet with great favor.

The delegates at Annapolis were confined by their instructions to considerations of commerce. But they unanimously agreed that "the power of regulating trade is of such comprehensive extent, and will enter so far into the general system of the Federal Government, that, to give it efficacy, and to obviate questions and

doubts concerning its precise nature and limits, may require a correspondent adjustment of other parts of the
federal system." [15] In short, the exigencies of the times
demanded that questions of commercial and of political
adjustment be treated together in a national way. The
whole system of government required revision if the
country was to be rescued from the "delicate and critical" situation [16] into which it had fallen. To meet the
problem the Annapolis delegates proposed that a Convention be called with representatives from all the states
"to meet at Philadelphia on the second Monday in
May," 1787.

It was for the very purpose of bringing order into
commercial affairs that the Convention had been called.
Its avowed object was to revise the Articles of Confederation. The Congress was to be given enough power to
ease the strangulation of commerce caused by state
tariff barriers and to nullify the insulating effect of England's trade policies. In addition it was expected that
something might be done to regulate bankruptcy, to
establish a stable medium of exchange, to impose a check
upon paper money, and to arrest legislation which permitted debtors to avoid their contractual obligations.
The questions of commerce which at any time are to
the front depend upon the exigencies of the times; and
the expectations of the event just ahead encompassed
all the economic problems that were current.

A threat to the very existence of "the American experiment" was in the air. A hard experience had shown that neither single governments nor states banded into an impotent league could suffice in an emergency. It was only through an undivided authority and a single plan that commerce could be employed to reorganize the national economy. The gloom which hung over the political situation could, in the words of Madison, be relieved "only by a hope that so select a body would devise an adequate remedy for the existing and prospective evils so impressively demanding it." [17]

3. *Young Men at Philadelphia*

The call had gone out for the gathering at Philadelphia. It had been prompted by the acuteness of the economic situation which the "depression of 1785" had thrown into relief.[18] A number of commercial questions had to be answered and the breach in the economy caused by the separation from Great Britain had to be repaired. Under other circumstances the action might have developed upon the political plane; and the Fathers might have been content to promote a "new deal" within the framework of an established order. But in matters of state the Confederation had failed; and "the impropriety of delegating to one body of men"—the existing Congress—broad powers to shape the economy of the country was evident.[19] So the duress of pressing events imposed upon the Convention a radical task of

political construction; and matters of commercial policy
had to await the contrivance of an adequate instrument
of government. But structure was shaped to the functions which the national authority was to perform; and,
if politics had the leading part in the play, economics
had its role back-stage to help the drama along.

Thus delegates—intent upon the problems of the times
and not unmindful of personal and sectional interests—
were cast in the role of nation-builders. The Revolution
had left the creation of a nation half-accomplished; the
Constitutional Convention was its necessary complement. The members came into Convention "to amend"
the Articles of Confederation; but once in session the
spirit of thoroughgoing reform proved contagious. And
in direct disregard of their official instructions, they remained to create a constitution designed "to form a
more perfect Union."

The Fathers, who drew up the new instrument of
government, were for the most part young men. Their
average age was forty-three—a year less than that of the
signers of the Declaration of Independence—and half of
their number had not yet passed beyond the thirties.
Like the signers of the older document they were English colonials by birth; but unlike them they were
Americans rather than citizens of Virginia, Massachusetts, or South Carolina. They had spent their forma-
tive years under the impulse of the separation from
Great Britain, and the war had given them a national

consciousness. To these men the colonies even when called States were less than sovereign; an authority had to be found to fill the place left vacant by King and Parliament; the national allegiance which had been lost had to be replaced.

Youth looks forward, not backward, and the feeling that the Constitution must be written in terms of the future runs as a leit-motif through the debates. James Wilson proclaimed that the "Government we are to form" will affect not only "the present generation of people and their posterity" but also "the whole Globe"; and admitted that "he was lost in the magnitude of the object." Madison stressed time and again the importance of "national and permanent views" and the need for a realization that what might "not be expedient at the present time may be so hereafter." And Benjamin Franklin's metaphor of the rising sun, drawn from the image painted on the President's chair, is an expression of a hopeful look towards the course ahead.[20] The young men of 1787—the Fathers of today [21]—were concerned with what lay ahead for themselves and their successors.

The men who gathered in the State House at Philadelphia were of many occupations. Among them were planters, physicians, lawyers, men of commerce, and representatives of the moneyed interest. Some had served in the Revolution and many had taken an active part in the politics of the Confederation.[22] All were men of substance and standing in their communities.

The Convention did not lack for lawyers. At least thirty-three of the delegates had experienced legal training and many more had read law extensively.[23] It was too much an affair of its own age to be unmarked by dialectic for the sake of dialectic. But, all in all, the spirit of legalism sat but lightly on the gathering. It was not interested in careful legal distinctions or in a "display of theory" that was "fitter for the schools." Although both had known some study in the law, the bent of Alexander Hamilton was towards political economy, and that of the more bookishly inclined James Madison to the realistic necessities of government.

It was in dominance an assembly of moneyed men cast in the role of nation-builders.[24] As luck and design would have it the commercial group had a representation out of all proportion to their numbers.[25] As men of experience they knew the evils of a depreciated paper currency, of the havoc wrought by local tariff barriers, of the futility of the attempts of the several states to regulate the intercourse which flowed across their borders, of the hazard to commerce in an unpaid public debt, and of the demoralization which attended the want of respect for the general government. They were conscious, too, of the plight of the country, keenly sensitive to the obstacles which lay in the way of the encouragement of manufactures, and ever watchful to guard commercial and sectional interests. As creditors of the government and persons with an interest in the rising system of commerce they were called upon to establish a national state.

They had the theories of their class and age as to how the wealth of the nation was to be promoted. They were intent upon incorporating notions that were sound to their own understanding into a durable instrument of government. They looked ahead—and did not neglect the problems of their own day. They sought the general welfare—through a public policy which seemed reasonable to gentlemen of substance. They became statesmen—without ceasing to be moneyed men.

The Constitution which they wrote is a product of the occasion, of the delegates, and of social vision. It is a collection of measures designed to meet a particular crisis; it is an expression of the prevailing ways of thought; it is a recognition of the interests which were current. It is the product of a political realism which enlisted section, class, and group in the service of the national state. It lives with the breath of the late Eighteenth Century—yet it has endured.

· III ·

The Language of the Fathers

---

1. *The Rule of Art*

IT IS easier to read the words than to sense the meaning of the Constitution. The document is written in the idiom of the late Eighteenth Century; and verbal currency passes most uncertainly between the generations.

A language is the verbal expression of a culture. As the things, the activities, and the ideas which make it up change, the diction of a people makes its accommodation. Words quickly shed old meanings and take on fresh ones; verbal concepts get newly filled with the stuff of everyday life; and idioms old and new come to reflect novel twists in thought-ways among the folk. One is prone to assume that, when words abide, meanings remain; yet some fifteen decades of cultural change —and their restless impact upon the language—lie between us and the words of the Constitution. We are doomed, unless we make a heroic attempt to get back

into a world which is gone, to read the classic document in the light of a later understanding.

The first aid in times of verbal perplexity is the dictionary. There something at least of the territory over
which words are allowed to roam can be discovered.
And even though the way of the lexicon is by synonym
and quotation—a revelation of the unknown in terms of
the unknown—the boundaries by which words were
pent in can be roughly blocked out. A dictionary, however, is not an objective mirror of contemporary usage.
It is rather a conventional aid to understanding which
has had its distinctive development.

The dictionary had its origin within the genteel
studies. It was an expression of the usage to be found
in polite literature; its quotations, never quite abreast of
the day, came largely from the English classics. It was
still something of a closed club of words; the matter of
taste—sometimes even the whims of the editor [1]—determined admission to its narrow circle. In the Eighteenth
Century the democratic notion of an objective and comprehensive picture of the speech of a people had not
yet found articulate expression. Words of ordinary life
or of trade and traffic—save as use by some master of
literature had made them canonical—were just being
admitted to the select ranks. There were, to be sure,
dictionaries and dictionaries,[2] and some had gone further than others in the descent from the drawing-room [3]
to the market-place. But even with the best—or the

most vulgar—of them, the scant lines need to be sup-
plemented by the stuff of treatise, pamphlet and broadside. All through the century the lexicographer's trade
was a handicraft to be practiced by an artisan and his
helpers; the collective enterprise for the systematic
record of the living speech of a people in its comprehensive pattern of variegated detail belonged to the
future.

The merchant in his business is omnipresent on the
stage of the Eighteenth Century, and his speech made
its way into even the most literary of dictionaries.
Although many terms of art and manufacture are
omitted,[4] much can be learned about the usages of trade
—as well as the learned editor's low opinion of the ways
of tradesmen—from Samuel Johnson. An entry into one
lexicon usually won admission into others; for words
and definitions were freely copied and no collection
seems to have been exclusive as against others of its
kind. Even the most complete tome fell short of a glossary of mercantile usage.

But each title page at least—which gave to blurb a
more enduring mortality than the modern jacket—proclaimed the distinction of the exhibition of words which
followed;[5] and here and there appeared a volume addressed to a particular clientele. In 1759, for example,
there was published a dictionary "peculiarly adapted to
Instruction and Improvement of those who had not had
the benefit of a learned or literary education."[6]

In these volumes a language quite unlike ours intro-
duces us to another world of affairs. Art reflects the contemporary approach to all that today we call industry.
It is impossible to describe the ways by which the Eighteenth Century made its living without a monotonous
reiteration of the word. Art is, simply and fundamen-
tally, "an abstract or metaphysical term"; it implies "a
collection of certain rules from observation and experience, by which anything may be performed or any
end obtained." But words, unless they are carefully
watched, have a habit of enlarging their confines; and
art, which was the act of acquiring—through being "used
promiscuously by authors for want of affixing certain
ideas to their words"—becomes the thing acquired.
Hence the word comes to refer to "a trade, cunning,
artfulness, speculation," [7] and to connote "all that is
performed by the Wit and Industry of a Man." [8]

A term so comprehensive has to be broken down for
everyday use. It became customary to refer to the
mechanical, the liberal, and the fine arts. The mechanical arts are "such as require more of the Labour of the
Hand or Body than of the Mind," or "make use of
mechanics to obtain their end." The liberal arts—and
sciences—are "those which consist in the application and
exercise of the mind, and are noble and genteel—such as
Grammar, Rhetorick, Musick, Physick, Mathematicks."
The composer, the sculptor, the painter, the man-of-
letters, who fabricated wares to appeal to the taste, were

still craftsmen, rather than creative aesthetes. Their trades were severally devoted to the cultivation of such as were fine [9] among the arts. The word has survived in its most genteel form; but art, however vulgar or refined, was in the Eighteenth Century man's activity, in a studied discipline, toward an appointed end.[10]

The arts were plied in a society of handicrafts just beginning to be transformed by the magic of invention. The names of tools and of trades abound in the lexicons; but terms of current technology carry an alien flavor. An engine is "a military machine"; an instrument compounded of "wheels, screws, levers . . . united and conspiring together" to produce a result "that could not be easily effected otherwise." [11] A machine is a "piece of workmanship . . . composed with art . . . made to produce motion, so as to save either time or force," and machinery, in "dramatic and heroic poetry," is the "part which the deities, angels, or demons perform," in solving "some knotty difficulty." [12] It is emerging from literature to ordinary life to be "an engine of which the several parts are set in motion by some principle contained in itself." [13] The disturbing series of events, many decades later to be called "the industrial revolution," [14] was well under way. America, as well as England, had its amateurs who spent their leisure time upon "projects"; [15] but as yet all such words of art are still untouched by the notion of mechanical power.

Art demanded artists of its own varied kind. An

artisan—a word not yet admitted to more select lexicographic company—is a rather low fellow, an unskilled
mechanic, manufacturer, or tradesman. The word is
"properly applied to those professors of trades which
require the least exercise of the understanding." An
artificer, on the contrary, at first "one by whom anything is made" or a "practiser of any mechanic business,"[16] has aristocratically become "a practitioner of
some skilled trade, a maker, a creator, an artist."[17] But
other words, with the same stress upon "the doing by
rule," had appeared to give more graphic identity to the
activity. A craftsman, or handicraftsman—a word passing into disfavor—is anyone who makes his living ply-
ing a "trade of skill."[18] A mechanic is an artisan, especially "a person employed in one of the meaner arts."[19]

In all probability the last word of the group to appear was manufacturer. As a reflection of the moving
ways of trade, it was undergoing a swift change of reference. It was, at first, a term for a man who made
things with his hands; it next passed on to a person who
"works up a natural production into an artificial commodity"; and at last it came to mean an enterpriser who
"keeps great numbers of men to work on any particular
commodity." As yet business had not emerged to corrupt a reputable word with fresh significance.[20]

In terms of finance the same note of alien usage is in
evidence. Coin, or money, was "pieces of metal, stamped
with some mark or image, whose value was fixed by

public authority." Credit was no more than the trust reposed in the debtor for later payment. A distinction prevailed between "the real money that every people have current among them" and "an imaginary money, or money of accompt, to which the real has relation." But as yet credit was not the name for this fictitious specie; nor had it usurped the place of money, become a distinctive institution, and given rise to the credit economy. A bank is still a "common repository" wherein persons agree to keep their "cash to be always ready at their call or direction, either to improve it or to keep it secure." A banker is still a tradesman, who trafficks in money, and gives his note for what he secures. Although the letter of exchange is well-established, a bank-bill is still a promissory note given by the bank for money placed there.[21]

The idea of authority was still very much alive. A plethora of terms attests the prevalence of the public regulation of commerce and the trades. "Rule," once "an instrument by which lines are drawn," has by political analogy become "a canon or precept by which thoughts or actions are directed." The term "regulate" still reflects the etymological purity of "the rule"; its shades of meaning run in a string of infinitives from "to square, rule, frame, or direct," through "to govern or guide, to discipline or instruct" and on "to settle, or fix, or decide or determine." And, to rise to the abstraction, regulation is "a rule or order prescribed by a superior for the proper management of some affair." Its domain was the art of politics, "the first part of economy"; [22] and consisted in "the well-governing" of "the affairs of state, for the maintenance of public safety, order, tranquility, and morals." [23]

Politics, far from a thing apart, had its approved ends. Weal, a state of happiness, had created "wealth" as the material means to its realization.[24] And wealth, forgetful of its instrumental character, had become possessions such as "money, sheep, horses, merchandise, land," and "all sorts of riches" quite worth while in themselves. So the opulence of the nation, "a state abounding in all the conveniences and ornaments of life," has come to be the objective of national policy.[25]

It is all very remote from our world—in activity, in process, in idea.

2. *The Vocabulary of Trade*

The same mark of a long time ago clings to the vocabulary of trade. For all their wisdom the Fathers could not anticipate the speech of the distant future; the judicial terms of a century and a half later were quite beyond their linguistic reach. In thought, in action, in resort to parchment their choice was limited to the words at hand and by prevailing usage in respect to those words.

To them business was a word out of reach. Its

etymology makes its eighteenth-century meaning clear enough. It had—in days when spelling was less regimented than today—ceased to be spelled with a "y"; but its content was still "busy-ness." A poet might make his love for her an all-consuming business; a critic might make it his business to lash the faults of others; and a disciple of Christ might plead that he "must be about his Master's business." In colloquial terms "to do a man's business" was still "a low and familiar phrase for killing, destroying, or ruining him." As set down in the dictionaries business was a general term that had reference to whatever one found to be busy about.[26]

Business had long been "an affair," "a subject of action," "a matter in question," "a serious engagement." [27] It was coming to be a term for employment or "anything that is the calling or occupation of a person." Although it was clearly on the make the word carried no connotation of concern with pecuniary matters, was still without generic significance, and had not yet been exalted to the rank of an abstraction.[28] The word roamed over no such lordly province as today.

The word "industry" was hardly within closer reach. The term was there, to be sure. It described a quality of ant and bee which man might well emulate; it was one of the cardinal virtues of a rising industrial Puritanism. An idle brain was the devil's workshop; and the provident man was enjoined by parson, squire, and almanac towards thrift, industry, and sobriety. In the dictionaries it is repeatedly associated with diligence, painstaking, assiduity. It is "the constant application of the mind or exercise of the body."

A slight shift in meaning can be found as far back as 1713. An eminent and outrageous author points out that although diligence and industry are used "promiscuously," there is a difference in meaning. For "industry implies more painstaking . . . a thirst after gain . . . an indefatigable desire of ameliorating one's condition." [29] But, even though the motive of profit had begun to command the meaning of the word, a century later found it little changed. As late as 1827 it was defined as "the exertion of the human faculties and powers to accomplish some desirable end." Still "no very marked line" was "drawn in common language, or by political economy, between industry and labor," save that "industry generally implies more superintendence and less bodily exertion." [30] At the expulsion from Eden, the curse of toil had been laid on the human race by a displeased Jehovah. In 1787 "industry" was the lot of man —to earn his bread by the "sweat of his brow." [31] As yet no decree of usage had come to cloud and to enlarge the pristine meaning of an obvious everyday word. [32]

Nor had manufacture as yet attained verbal eminence. As "any sort of commodity made by the work of the hands of things that are naturally produced," it covered the processing of agricultural products for use. Wheat ground into flour, hides cured and worked into jackets

and shoes, vegetable or animal fiber spun and woven at
home, tobacco sun-cured and prepared for pipe or as
snuff—all these were "manufactures." Thus farmers—as
well as the "laboring poor" of the great cities—were
manufacturers. The word was still a name, not for an
activity apart but for an aspect of the art of husbandry.

Articles of manufacture, however, might be intended
for sale. Household wares and goods "worked up" by
skilled artisans were produced for "commerce." As their
importance in the national economy grew, the word
manufacture drifted from country to city; but even at
the end of the century it still carried the connotation of
"forming by hand." A standard dictionary of the period
reveals the swift transformation of the word at the impact of industrial change from the fashioning of a ware
by hand, to the "workhouse where several artificers are
employed in the same kind of work." [33]

In 1787 the word was on its way. It was being used
by some writers to describe a type of occupation different alike from agriculture and from merchandising;
but such a usage was attended with difficulties. It entailed careful definition, lengthy explanation, or elaborate qualification.[34] For in the Eighteenth Century
manufacture was the supplementary activity necessary
to make things "naturally produced" by agriculture fit
for consumption. If the producer worked the product
up for his own use, the process was part of subsistence
agriculture. If the substance was to be disposed of in the

market, the labor expended to "meliorate" and transform it into a "finer" ware was an adjunct to commerce. The word was still in an amorphous state; manufacture was only tentatively becoming the generic name for the collective enterprise by which wares are fashioned for sale.

But the lack of the familiar term is not the want of a word. If the Eighteenth Century did not anticipate modern usage in the words "business," "industry," and "manufacture," it did have terms of its own with which to describe the seamless web of activities by which commodities are fashioned for use, men earn their livings, and nations acquire wealth. In 1787 three words of different stock—traffick, trade, and commerce—were at hand for this multiple verbal duty. Each was suited by shade and variation to its own distinctive usage; yet each in its own right was capable of a verbal coverage almost as comprehensive as the prevailing economic order.[35]

Of the three, traffick was the oldest. It was of lowly origin, and had come to be vulgar in repute. As a verbal *émigré* from France, it had come into use early in the Sixteenth Century when the itinerant peddler was a fellow of low cunning and devious ways and exchange was tolerated only along the fringes of respectable society. One had traffick with mendicant, huckster, merchant, hussy, and evil spirit. Although during the Eighteenth Century the word came to mean "trade," large or small, "merchandising" and even "commerce," the ancient moral stigma still remained. And, as a verb, it meant "to trade meanly or mercenarily." [36]

In ordinary use it covered, like trade and commerce, all dealings in wares. Yet it alone was used to connote matters which should not be made the subject of trade. It never quite cast off the taint of shabbiness, or freed itself from the implication of being sinister or illicit. As the activities which it described became more and more respectable, trade and commerce came increasingly to do duty for it; and by 1787 it had been driven into quite low verbal company. In the Convention trade and commerce are used frequently and interchangeably; yet traffic is used only in relation to the slave trade.[37]

The origin of trade is unknown. It seems to have come into England from the Hanseatic Towns in the Fourteenth Century. If it really lacked for a Latin root, in *trado* it quickly fitted itself out with a reputable pedigree. Its primitive form was tred, tread, trade, or some other way of saying track or footstep. By 1550 it had come to mean "manner of life," "course of action," "mode of procedure," or "habitual course of doing something." A century later it had taken to itself the meaning of a regular occupation.[38] But as craftsmen became manufacturers, and commodities were produced for markets, the word obligingly added new content. Trade came to be the "Art of Getting, Preparing and Exchanging Things Commodious for Humane Necessi-

ties and Convenience." [39] As, however, it came to denote the fashioning and vending of goods for other
goods or money, it narrowed its coverage of employment. By 1755 it was no longer used for activities which
required "constant exercise of the mind," and was especially applied to the "mechanical" pursuits in contradis-
tinction to the "liberal arts and learned professions." [40]
The "master-manufacturer" and the great merchant, as
well as the lowly artisan and small shopkeeper, were "in
trade," for trade had come to encompass all those activities that were "manual or mercantile."

In its development the idea of profit comes to the
front. A number of careful lexicographers read into the
term "to act merely for money," and Kenrick describes
a "trader" as "one long used in the methods of money-
getting." In the economy of the time fabrication and
sale were inseparable; and in its generic meaning it had
come to denote "the same with commerce, consisting
in buying, selling and exchanging of commodities, bills,
money." [41]

The word "commerce" is of more exalted rank. It
came into English, not by way of some vulgar tongue,
but directly from the Latin. It is, in etymology, a "buying together," and from the beginning it signified a bartering of wares, an engagement in the general practice
of merchandising, and all the arrangements appertaining
thereto.[42] This primary core of meaning is set down by
Benjamin Martin, Samuel Johnson, and William Rider

just after the middle of the Eighteenth Century; it is repeated by William Kenrick and Thomas Dyche, whose dictionaries appeared about the time of the Declaration of Independence; and it is perpetuated by Thomas Sheridan, William Scott, and William Perry, whose tomes were published in the last decade of the century.[43] Its prestige, however, had carried it far from its original base. Almost all the dictionaries of the times set down as a secondary meaning such a miscellany of terms as "conversation," "society," and "intercourse." Between its original core of meaning and its periphery lies a vast territory.[44]

Its sprawling domain and multiplicity of meaning are explored by all the reputable dictionaries of the period, popular and literary. The smaller and more popular of them are content to identify the word with trade or traffic; and to limit their definition to these naked words. The more pretentious tomes make excursions in various directions to find out the boundaries of the unknown domain. Dyche sets down "dealing," adds "conversation by word or letter," and reaches out to "correspondence of every kind." Barclay, with an eye to mundane matters, ventures more carefully from his verbal base. He sets it down that commerce is "the exchange of commodities," or "the buying and selling of merchandise both at home and abroad," and adds "in order to gain a profit or increase the conveniences of life." He makes the concern of both "trade" and "com-

merce" the "manufacture and vending of merchandise."
Samuel Johnson, as is his wont, quickly leaves the
everyday world and takes an extended literary flight. In
his quotations a "commerce with the rest of the world"
may be "without the use of silver coin"; "instructed
ships shall sail to quick commerce"; and "commerce"—
seemingly another name for the communion of saints—
exists between "God and us."

But boundaries were not easily marked out. English
has an affinity for borrowed terms and likes to have
handy a number of words with which to express an
idea. Usage is forever modifying its decrees; and the
exuberant verbal growth during the century makes futile any final judgments in jurisdictional disputes. Trade,
traffic, and commerce, in general identical in content,
were usually distinguished only in ethical flaw or social
prestige. Only lexicographers meticulous in their diction
attempted to endow them with subtle shades of meaning. Samuel Johnson declares that "formerly trade was
used of domestic and traffick of foreign commerce," [45]
and implies that the three words have no essential difference. Barclay insists that "trade" had not lost the
color of "domestic" interchange of commodities, but
"seems to imply the manufacturing and vending within
ourselves." He feels that "commerce" and not "trade"
should be called upon properly to denote "negociating
with other countries." [46] But no other dictionary seems
to find this distinction necessary. As "trade" had moved

forward from occupation or calling to exchange, so "commerce" had moved backward from market-place to manufacture for profit. It was all eminently logical, for in the economy of the time fabrication and sale were all but inseparable.[47] It was the wideness of its domain which forbids a narrow definition of its content.

But as an aspect of the economy of the nation or as a province of government "commerce" was pent within sharper limits. In a letter to her husband Abigail Adams, proud in the possession of a cow and a garden, writes, "but whortleberries and milk we are not obliged to commerce for." Such a distinction between that which was bought and that which was produced on the place permeates the literature of the period. The American might make his own shoes, grind his own grain, process his raw materials into articles for his own "farm hands"; but if he fashioned wares for the market, his efforts were directed towards commerce. The expression "in commerce" was habitually employed to designate shop, mill, factory, or foundry whose products were intended for sale. A grist-mill, a sawmill, an iron works, a shoe factory were in commerce; and such persons as sold their own services for hire were engaged in the commercial callings.[48] The manufactures, whose wares went to market, and the staple crops of agriculture were "in commerce." The age knew only two ways of making a living, the direct application of labor to land, and the making and exchange of wares. In the world of the Fathers the agricultural economy of self-sufficiency and the commercial, or the moneyed, economy stood in sharp contrast. In their minds the boundaries of commerce extended to the frontiers of the domestic economy.

A rule of status has never been imposed upon the tongue of a people. An axiom of language holds that where activities are continuous, words tend to be contagious; and another has it that when things change, the old term obligingly goes along. As time passes, nouns, forgetful that they are the names of things, tend to grow up, or to drift off. To such a liberty, which allows words to roam and to come to rest and makes language immune to the blueprint, the noblest word of trade was granted indulgence. Commerce—free from the moral taint that attached to traffic and blessed with the charm of elegance—[49] was far along that respectable road. In 1787 all actions or dealings made with an eye to the market were "in commerce."

3. *The Prestige of Commerce*

Here is a word reputable, imposing, elegant, even romantic. For three centuries it was intimately associated with the most dynamic aspects of European culture. At the beginning of the Sixteenth Century, it had been caught up into the heroic activities of the great age of exploration. Its verbal dominion had advanced with the desire to commerce with Cathay and Hindoostan, with the journey of Vasco da Gama around the Cape of Good Hope, with the venture of Christopher Columbus, as an emissary of their Catholic Majesties of Spain, into the western seas beyond the Azores. It was the desire to "practice commerce" that led to the establishment of factories at Pondicherry and Calicut, that gave names to the "Gold Coast" and the "Slave Coast" of Africa in the likeness of the wares for which each was famous.

In the New World "the pursuit of commerce" took its own course. The poorly armed natives, the indigenous products little touched by art, and the impact of western civilization upon primitive culture conspired to create distinctive usages for trade. In the Americas it was not necessary to bargain for trading privileges with the inhabitants; there was no Great Mogul or Celestial Emperor to restrain the avidity of the white man to the seemly methods of Christian intercourse. The Age of Exploration was merged into the Age of Colonization; and the nations of Europe struggled with each other to exploit new territory and to bring home exotic products. The flood of gold, goods, and precious wares from the Indies of West and East transformed domestic commerce. With amazing rapidity intercourse reduced the arrangements of the feudal establishment to vestiges; and commerce and the national state arose and flourished together. The word had, from the contagion of its dynamic world, taken to itself a color and a richness which it is hard to sense today.

In the language of the times "commerce" had come to be a glorious domain. It included trade, manufacture, and the staples; comprehended all arrangements which lay outside the domestic economy; and invited the solicitude of ministers of state.[50] Its virtues and vices were paraded, extolled, and debated in tome and pamphlet; the contagion spread from polemic to poem. A bard sensitive to its cultural implications explained:

"For Commerce, though the Child of Agriculture,
   Fosters his parent, who else must sweat to toil
   And gain but scanty fare." [51]

Another, conscious only of what it was doing to the ancient ways of the people, set it down that:

"From art more various are the blessings sent,
   Wealth, commerce, honor, liberty, content.
   Yet these each other's power so strong contest
   That either seems destructive of the rest.
   Where wealth and freedom reign, contentment fails;
   And honor sinks where commerce long prevails." [52]

And in panegyric and eulogy "commerce" is hailed and damned as the hero or villain in the piece of man's progress.[53] As yet this fresh meaning has not found full entry into the lagging dictionaries of the time.

As early as the accession of George III, William Rider, more than usually sensitive to the prevailing cli-

mate of opinion, could not keep the note of exuberance
from his objective lines. To "commerce" the country
owes such categories of national wealth as "the number
of our people, shipping, colonies, and riches, the value
of our landed estates, the strength of our island, and the
respectable figure it makes in the eyes of all the world."
The persons "who shall form any plan to render our
trade more extensive and profitable"—in his lexicographic eyes—"are worthy immortal fame." And, in
the spirit of his day, he extolls "this great view in the
society" which makes for promoting arts, sciences, and
commerce; is "astonished at the *eclat* with which patriotism appears in this island"; and like the good Englishman that he is prays "for its perpetuity." In his dictionary, art, trade, manufacture, whatnot, have only a
descriptive definition; in short and "in fine"—as it would
then have been put—it was "commerce" which comprehended all those activities which made for the greatness
and the glory of the realm.[54]

It is all but impossible in our own age to sense fully
its eighteenth-century meaning. The Eighteenth Century did not separate by artificial lines aspects of a culture which are inseparable. It had no lexicon of legalisms
extracted from the law reports in which judicial usage
lies in a world apart from the ordinary affairs of life.
Commerce was then more than we imply now by business or industry. It was a name for the economic order,
the domain of political economy, the realm of a com-

prehensive public policy. It is a word which makes trades, activities and interests an instrument in the culture of a people. If trust was to be reposed in parchment, it was the only word which could catch up into a single comprehensive term all activities directly affecting the wealth of the nation.

A dictionary, however, is not even in verbal matters a court of last resort. Its pages do not embody living usage but only its reflection. It selects words, garners their meanings, explores their confines, and imposes upon current diction its regimented lines. Its way of abstraction tears away verbal symbols with only a fragment of the tentacles which bind them to their linguistic habitat. Its lagging entries cannot keep up with all that an active people in a changing culture are doing to words. A complement demands a further exploration into the world of activity—of event and problem, of policy and dialectic—which shaped words to its requirements. For it is the stress of the times which makes the words.

· IV ·

The Paths for the Mind

1. *The Course of Human Events*

AN AGE differs from another in the ways of thought. It has its own interval in the stream of history; its act in the drama of time has its own theme, its own setting, its own characters. It has its own matters of public interest to bother about; it gives its own stamp to the passing system of values and taboos; its perspective upon affairs obeys its own decrees. It puts together things which in another period would lie apart; it stumbles over associations which in another era would be obvious. In the Eighteenth Century, through all the domain of statecraft, there were beaten paths for the mind.

A clash of interests, of arms, and of words has gone resounding down the century. It had all begun long ago in the unobtrusive impact of strange events upon a culture which professed to be established. A new learning—masquerading as a renaissance—brought knowledge and doubt to every affair and in every domain challenged authority. A printing press, a novel anatomy, a new world, a reformed religion, a system of natural law, a money economy made their stealthy entrance and proceeded unwelcomed to find places for themselves within a familiar culture.

The medieval world was, to the souls which tarried in it, a place of order. From pope to peasant every man had his place in the great Christian commonwealth, and was expected to live in accordance with the station in life to which God had appointed him. A hierarchy—ecclesiastic and feudal—offered regimentation to a placid society disturbed by the doughty deeds of a small privileged group. But to the medieval mind the approved pattern of position and conduct were more real than the actual departures by erring brethren; and even such commotion as prelate and prince might create was held within the grooves of custom. But the intrusion of new devices, new ideas, and new values was too much for the ancient regime of fief and field, of vassal and lord, of mitre and surplice. Here was far more of novelty than the culture could assimilate without shock.

A newness had come into every domain of life to release creative energy—and to touch off conflict. A dogmatic learning had to make place for newly discovered facts. A revealed religion had to patch up a truce with individual freedom. Conduct directed by novel circumstance could no longer accord with accepted standards. The drama, painting, and poetry refused to conform to established art forms. Everywhere the surging activities of a new life broke the molds in which it was expected to run.

Men sought to make the most of newer opportunities. They reached out towards the El Dorados that lay at the ends of the earth. As they did, the medieval peoples of Spain, France, and Holland became rival political states; and even England, a large sheep pasture on the fringe of Christendom, awoke to take its place in the sun. A series of wars—for the spoils of new worlds—created nations and brought a spirit of nationalism. England struggled with Spain and Holland over gold and spices, over the territory of America and the Indies, and over the true religion. Shortly before the contest with the Colonies it had triumphed over France in the New World.

For foreign wars could not use up all the energy generated by cultural conflict. Although the issue lay on too many fronts to be clearly defined, high emotions provoked interminable verbal conflict but ran too deep for articulate expression. In Spain a violent outpouring of new energy left a nation once certain of its destiny headed for nowhere in particular. In England the turbulence of spirit and event found vent in domestic struggle. A revolution, a civil war, a protectorate, a restoration of monarchy, and a silent revolution which occupied the better part of a century, provided not a settlement but a parliamentary instrument through which the issues were transferred to the political arena.

The American Revolution, as much a civil war as a struggle to throw off the yoke of George III, was but part of the larger conflict. It was, at least in pamphlet and polemic, fought almost as vigorously in England as in America.[1] In several of the Colonies, under cover of the struggle, rights of the people were wrung from ancient establishments. And hardly were the labors of the Fathers completed before in France the forces of change, held overlong in leash, were to break in violent revolution.

In the making of national policy the conflict took a more orderly course. A feudal system, through the rise of monarchy, had been converted into an agrarian state. The king, with parliament and ministry as irritant and guide, was seeking to enhance the greatness of his realm. In England a flood of gold had provided the wherewithal for a money economy; a fishing fleet had, by way of piracy, grown up into a merchant marine; and the itinerant peddler had come up in the world to the position of merchant prince. A new interest had arisen to dispute control of crown, legislature and policy with the landed gentry. Against the traditional view that the wealth of the nation lay in the land, it was boldly asserted that England's treasure lay in foreign trade.[2] Thus it was that the commercial interest had to wage an aggressive fight on a double front—to command a domestic polity long harnessed to agrarian ends and to shape a foreign policy towards a winning of competitive markets.

From the earliest times the power of the state to regulate was taken for granted. All through the Middle Ages—in church, fief, manor, and market—it had been established upon the firmest foundations. The medieval commonwealth was a loose agglomeration of communities, large and small, in which individuals severally were members one of another. A spirit of benevolent paternalism prevailed. A stewardship with exacting responsibilities was imposed upon "the powers that be" which were ordained of God. It was not always clear what power was rightful or which one of conflicting authorities had been properly constituted—nor were men always in agreement about God's ordinance. But throughout Christendom the rightfulness of authority and the duty of obedience were unquestioned. This impulse toward authoritative control—an aspect of the common sense of the times—marked church and feudal system; it was taken for granted in the "self-government" of manor, guild, and voluntary association. As the feudal monarchy gave way to the national state, the authority to make rules for the trades endured.

The system of control could not escape the stress of change. As the decades passed, as new wares and new markets appeared, traffic swelled into a mighty stream. It was impossible to hold commerce within grooves carved out for it. The status of labor, the common callings,[3] the fabrication of important wares,[4] and the usages of the market had passed from guild or municipality, and were under the control of the state. As yet half a century was to pass before the word individualism was to appear in the language,[5] and to most of the Founding Fathers the term *laissez-faire* [6] would have been unintelligible.

Here and there a protestant was saying [7]—in words not yet quite articulate—that trade ought to be allowed to carve out its own routes. But no one was insisting that competition be permitted to find its own plane or that commerce should be allowed to govern itself. The wisdom of particular policies might be questioned; their administration might be attended with neglect. But the principle of the subordination of individual and corporate activities to the wealth of the nation was not seriously disputed.

A struggle over policy was everywhere in evidence. It was concerned, not with the power of regulation—which was taken for granted—but with the objectives it should be made to serve. The gentility of England had once been of the land. The older foundations of public policy, far more deeply rooted in usage than in statute, had been rural. A general belief that land alone is the source of all wealth made common sense a defense of the agricultural interest. But entrenched as it was in vested law, the usages of the community, and intellectual repute, it could not stand unchallenged before the swift course of human events. There was flux in philosophy, science, theology, and even in music.[8] The mind, turned in upon itself during the Middle Ages, drove outward to new notions, new values, new ends for the state. A stream of diverse influences were working together to make of England a nation—and its claims were not to be denied.

As merchants acquired power, they were not loath to use it. A commercial interest was brought into the councils of the nation. As a result there developed—through a series of expediencies—a public policy to which later the name "mercantilism" was given.

2. Interests in the State

The state was the thing. In the Eighteenth Century it was no "brooding omnipresence in the skies," an abstraction outside of and above the realities which made it up. Nor had it yet become a super-policeman whose office it was to prevent force and fraud, and to allow the actors on the economic stage to play out their drama without interference. It was an affair of groups and interests, whose concerns must be promoted through its policies, and whose aspirations must be trimmed to the requirements of "the general welfare." [9] Hence no sharp line was drawn between the political and the economic order.[10] The state had the dominant role in matters of commerce, and a political economy of expedience had not yet been toned down into a mechanistic economics of principles.[11] It was among the first precepts of politics "to perceive the reciprocal dependence of trade and agriculture" and "their near connection with laws, morals, and all the business of government." This was "to look at the matter with the eye of a statesman and a philosopher." [12]

For it was the mode of the age to resolve the articulate political groups into the "agricultural" and the "commercial" or "trading" interest. "Agriculture or husbandry is the original source of most of our treasures," says Rider. It is "the great fountain for all materials for commerce, and . . . the articles of commerce must consequently endear themselves to those who trade in them, and render agriculture still more amiable in their eyes." He adds, quite gratuitously, that "it will always be good policy, to ease the land, to promote trade; and to encourage the trading interest, in order to promote the landed." A "politico-Commercial Geography of Europe" encompasses "a compendious and comparative view of the various productions, trades, manufactures, exportations, populousness, and power of the several potentates, republics, and states thereof" and includes "a brief survey of the commerce, magnitude, and people of their most considerable cities and towns." [13] As a name for a great interest in the state, commerce had come into a position of eminence in the vocabulary of public policy.

The logic of interests within the state was not far to seek. "The delicacy of a man's body," explains Adam Smith, "requires much greater provision than that of any other animal." Therefore "the whole industry of human life is employed, not in procuring the supply of our three humble necessities, food, clothes, and lodging, but in procuring the conveniences of it according to the nicety and delicacy of our taste. To improve and multiply the materials, which are the principal objects of our necessities, gives occasion to all the variety of the arts." [14]

Implicit in this statement lies the prevailing concept of the domains of Nature and Art. Nature produced the "necessities of life," "food, clothes, lodging"; but it was Art which supplied the "conveniences" that lifted life above mere animal existence. Agriculture came first "as subsistence is, in the nature of things, prior to conveniency and luxury" and "the industry which procures the former, must necessarily be prior to that which ministers to the latter." [15]

But as states grew more civilized and society less rude, a division of labor was established. Then, since a man's own labor can provide "but a very small part of a man's wants," the individual "supplies the far greater part of them by exchanging that surplus part of the produce of his own labour, which is over and above his own consumption, for such parts of the produce of other men's labour as he has occasion for. Every man thus lives by exchanging, or becomes in some measure a merchant, and the society itself grows to be what is properly a commercial society." [16]

The distinction of interests springs from the application of labor. "The annual labour of every nation is the fund which . . . supplies it with all the necessaries and conveniences of life." [17] If the labor was expended specifically on the land, the laborer was "in agriculture," the primary function of which was to produce the "necessities of life." But if the laborer's activity had to do with the "surplus produce of the country, or what is over and above the maintenance of the cultivators," then the laborer was "in commerce." [18] His toil, whether by "refining" the product through manufacture, or by facilitating the exchange of wares, added to the "conveniences" and "comforts" of life.[19] Here is reflected the harmony and the conflict of "the agricultural" and "the commercial" interest.

The landed interest was entrenched in habit, tradition, and value. The law, common sense, and public policy were on its side. The feudal system had left in its wake the notion that the land alone was productive; and the belief still persisted that agriculture produces substances and that manufacture only alters them. Adam Smith, an intelligent observer, states without equivocation that "the town, in which there neither is nor can be any reproduction of substances, may very properly be said to gain its whole wealth and subsistence from

the country." [20] Nor were the country gentry unwilling
to limit a term so useful to them in politics as production to their own activities.[21]

An important counter in the clash of interests was the
sensational discovery of "the laws of Nature." In an
attempt to understand the physical universe, Isaac Newton had bridged the gap between the earth and the
heavens by discovering that the very force which causes
the apple to fall holds the stars in their celestial courses.[22]
The thought of the age ran to Nature, to the laws of
Nature, and to Nature's god; and the idea of the uniformity and inevitability of Nature began to make its
way into ethics, economics, and politics. There appeared
a natural theology of deism; [23] and some person invented
for music a natural harmony.

Although it was fashioned to their cause, the landed
gentry in England were slow to turn such an intellectual resource to account.[24] In France, however, the
notion of the laws of Nature were seized upon by the
apologists for the agrarian interest, made to fortify
popular beliefs, and used in the fabrication of the doctrines of the Physiocrats.[25] In America, patriots in search
for a sanction to justify repudiation of an ancient allegiance to the English crown, found "the laws of Nature" a comfortable refuge; but they made little use of
them as a justification of the dominance of agriculture
in the national state. The idea was left to be appro-
priated; and the commercial interest converted it into a

system of natural laws for an economic order which had issued its declaration of independence from the political state.

But economic rebellion against political overlordship belonged to the future. In 1787 the paternalism of the government extended to agriculture and commerce; and its function was alike to promote their well-being and to reconcile their differences. Politics was still "the first part of economy." Its instrument was "public policy," [26] or "the laws, orders, and regulations" of "the government of any city or state" for "the maintenance of the public safety, order, tranquility, and morals." [27] And "police," a grand derivative, connoted all of "regulation or government" as "it respects the inhabitants of a country." [28]

In policy the conflicting interests of an economy were resolved; in the police the general welfare of the body politic was promoted.[29] As the commercial interests came into dominance, mercantilism was policy shaped to its requirements.

3. *The Matter of Domestic Polity*

Mercantilism—like all the intellectual creations of a commercial class—was opportunistic, practical, pragmatic. As a scheme for the promotion of trade at home and abroad it was never consciously formulated. It embodied no principles save those which emerged in its creation; it was the expression of no national policy except that which arose from its expediencies.

It was of the stuff of the times. In underlying idea, in circumstance to be met, in instrument to be used, in a national opulence to be attained, it was woven of eighteenth-century fabric. Among those in authority there might be differences as to what was wise; and adventitious events constantly brought shifts in policy. But statesmen and men of affairs lived within its atmosphere; and in their doings they had to follow the bent of the times.

A vague term for a slowly developing policy, mercantilism was a product of an alliance of the state and the commercial interest. The merchants—as adventurers, founders of chartered companies, and men of affairs— needed the government to break down domestic trade barriers, to establish sound commercial policies, to clear the seas of pirates, and to blaze open foreign markets with treaties and arms. The state found a helpful ally in the commercial group. Merchants, more than men of any other trade, helped to break down local allegiance and strengthen the crown. The need for royal revenue was insistent; [30] and the ports were points at which a toll could be taken on the mounting volume of passing traffic. A trade from overseas promised to fill the war chest and to increase the competitive strength of the nation.

A mutuality of interest linked political with mercantile affairs. The state became the dominant agent in the production of wealth. The welfare of the people hung upon the powers of the King and the wisdom of his ministers. The individual was a citizen of a political economy; the country was to be made rich; and in national opulence the loyal subject of His Majesty was to share. It thus required no serious departure from common sense to rationalize the mercantile interest as the wealth of the nation.

A number of ideas had gone into the making of the policy. A revolution had occurred in social and moral values; men could no longer be quite serious in their renunciation of the world, the flesh, and the devil. They reached out quite unashamed for the comforts and vanities of life; and the discipline of the Church over economic activities had been relaxed. It was even argued, openly and seriously, that "private vices," by creating a demand for the wares of trade, were "public virtues." [31] A local had given way to a national allegiance; the man from York was no longer a foreigner to the citizen of Bristol; they had both become Englishmen.[32] Even a staunch Colonial, such as Benjamin Franklin, spoke of "going home to England." The loyalty to state had been exalted above devotion to Church; and the medieval aspiration of a universal Christian commonwealth had given way to the spirit of competitive nationalism.[33]

Along two fronts the rising state had to assert its authority. It had to triumph over local autonomy and

it had to enhance its position among the nations of the
world. The one was the concern of domestic polity,
the other of foreign policy. Although they are complementary aspects of the same political adventure, the critic
and the expositor have given far less attention to the
internal than to the external policy of mercantilism.
Yet for centuries the trades had been made obedient to
the common good and their regulation was the continuance of an established tradition. The slow, solid,
pedestrian achievements of national policy in the domestic realm were alike foundation and complement to
glamorous endeavor that reached out overseas towards
wares, colonies, and empire.[34]

The domestic policy of mercantilism is a checkered
affair of accident and design, of control and leaving
alone. The sweep of change stripped from the guilds
their liveries, their monopolies of wares, and their control over their members. The growing stream of commerce was too strong for a municipal regulation shaped
to the necessities of petty trade. All over the land ancient
rule and custom were proving inadequate to the task
of control. The rising national state was quick to turn
such a situation to account. In the flux of an opportunistic policy it made shrewd use of strict regulation
and studied neglect. It employed its power as a prop to
local authority when the national advantage lay that
way. It allowed merchants to disregard local regulation,
trade to cut its own channels, and commerce to establish

its own usages when such a course promised the greater gain to the realm. It usurped the function once performed by guild, liveried company, and town. In statutes it sought to bring apprentices, artificers, and others under a single rule. It attempted to impose upon the activities concerned with wealth-getting a truly unified pattern. In this high endeavor it exercised no empty right of regulation; its police had everywhere the strength of the nation as its purpose.

A scheme of trade regulation, whose roots were grounded in the medieval past, was an aspect of polity. An ethical ban, which savors of the Middle Ages, still clung to a number of arts. The engrosser—a piratical ancestor of the grocer—willfully and maliciously bought up a commodity "to sell it again at an advanced price." The forestaller took up his station to intercept "customers as they go to market," and bought up "great quantities of provisions . . . only to raise their price." [35] The statutes against regrating, forestalling, and engrossing—with their traditional disapproval of merchandising—were to stand on the statute books of England until 1842.

But a bankrupt was even more of a public menace. He was a person whose perfidy is to be understood only against ethical norms for his conduct invented by country gentlemen. He· is one who is, or "pretends to be," unable to pay his debts, or "a trader" that "having gotten together other men's goods hides himself with

a design to defraud his Creditors"; or "one who, living
by buying and selling, hath got the goods of others in his
hands and concealeth himself from them." In its terms a
pecuniary lapse is a social sin,[36] and bad business judgment has not yet been distinguished from personal de-
falcation.[37]

A price is a point at which the maker of a ware meets
its user; and price, "the heart of the bargain," lay likewise at the center of regulation. The sweep of change
had confused the simple problems of just price; and
although regulation ran into novel difficulties, the control of prices—to the common good and the gain of the
realm—continued to be the part of statecraft. But an in-
herited authority was accommodated in practice to the
necessities of the rising competitive state. The dominance
of custom was broken by a relaxation of ancient restrictions; the nation became agent and end of public
control.

As price reflects the usages of the market, so wages
reflect the political attitude toward price. A belief long
prevalent had associated wages with the customary way
of life. In the national economy wages were beginning
to be thought of as an expense that might be help or
hindrance in the winning of foreign markets. It was
believed that the costs of wares produced for the wealth-
making export trade were made up of the costs of raw
materials plus the wages of the laborers who worked
them up. In a cottage type of manufacture, in which "a

capital charge" was absent or negligible, the final cost reflected wages paid. Hence it seemed plain that a regulation of the laborer's hire was the way to the prices which would win markets abroad. If the competition became severe—assuming the access of all nations to raw materials at the same price—the only recourse of policy was to force down wages. A market won was not to be abandoned, and therefore low wages were a national economy.

As a first principle of political economy such a belief was helped along by the opinion of the times. It required no intricate argument to demonstrate to squire, judge, or merchant that a national advantage lay in low wages and the pinch of poverty; and "everyone but an idiot" knew "that the lower classes must be kept poor or they will never be industrious." [38] An authority of the Eighteenth Century was led from axiomatic premises, by a peradventureless logic, to the inescapable conclusion that high wages, instead of stimulating the laborer to greater efforts, resulted only in the reduction of the number of working days.[39] The Scriptures, too, could be quoted as authority that "the poor ye have with you always." It was accordingly reason to set it down that a wage which represents a bare minimum of subsistence is for the good of the nation.[40]

An acceptance of subsistence as its measure states the political issues of wages. What should the masses be allowed to consume? What should they spend their money on? A group of writers wished to restrict the laborer to necessities, and to deny him the use of such "luxuries and superfluities" as "snuff, tea, ruffles, silks, and ribbands." Such an indulgence would increase the expenses of production, raise the cost of living, advance the prices of export wares, affect adversely the nation's balance of trade, and threaten the foundations of national wealth. It was especially to be abhorred if the luxuries were foreign in origin. Here is an idea that permeated far into public policy.[41] It helps to explain the acceptance of sumptuary acts which, with minute detail, regulated consumption, and for classes of the people put many wares of trade beyond the pale of the law. It explains, too, the prejudice against manufactures held by men who with pride in the domestic economy of self-sufficiency had doubts in the mercantile faith.

4. *And of Foreign Policy*

As national unity was sought at home, so national strength was the great objective of foreign policy. In the Sixteenth and Seventeenth Centuries great national states had arisen, ready at all times to have at each other with blockades, tariffs, and arms. War was an instrument of national policy and peace was an armed interlude in a series of trade wars. As yet the economy of King and Realm had not been separated. Measures of commercial import were tempered towards an increase in the royal revenues.

In the minds of ministers of state the regulation of trade was an exercise of the war power. A mercantile policy, as well as a ready militia, was a means of national defense. As, alternately through the Eighteenth Century, the arena was shifted from the battlefield to the legislature, troops were replaced by tariffs. In the attainment of an imperial autonomy the military arm and commerce were complementary instruments ready at all times for competitive use.

Idea and occasion combined to put a high national value upon a favorable balance of trade. The New World had brought commerce upon the political stage with a fanfare of trumpets. Its treasures had—by the way of the Spanish Main—yielded gold and silver, provided the wherewithal of a money economy, and made feasible an easy system of exchange. In East and West alike a traffic with the natives, in which the white man received far more than he gave, was a monopoly that invited national exploitation. To the popular mind the precious metals—which in an England without mines could be had only through the pursuits of piracy and commerce —were a special kind of wealth. They were exalted in the national economy as alone capable of filling the public treasury—the war chest—with bullion. A favorable balance of trade bore testimony to investment abroad and an enlargement of colonial possessions. The nation had embarked upon its quest of empire.

A favorable balance of trade, accordingly, became a pivot upon which public policy turned. A hang-over from the Middle Ages colored its initial statement. The belief that what one party to a trade gained the other lost still survived; it was lifted from the individual to become an axiom of the national economy. It followed that a nation must export more than it imported and that the favorable balance in specie was a net addition to opulence. In name and idea money was confused with capital and wealth. The precious metals had long ago become the stake in mercantile adventure. If piracy had lost caste, there was still policy to further an indirect quest for silver and gold. A nation must assiduously win its wealth at the expense of other nations. Its measures must encourage exports and discourage imports. Its statecraft, intent upon the national economy, must be shaped by the exigencies of military and commercial hostility.

By the end of the Eighteenth Century the cruder notions had been refined. Gold and silver were no longer national wealth but varied proportionately with it. The inflow of the precious metals was to be invited and their outflow discouraged. It therefore became a matter of primary concern to import cheap and bulky commodities and to export wares high in value. Exports were to leave the country only in a finished state; not wool but cloth, not cloth but cloth finished and dyed, was to go abroad. Conversely raw materials were in public policy the ideal imports. The gain to the nation was double. The low value of imports would lessen the debit; the use of domestic labor to fabricate materials for re-export would augment the credit; and the favorable balance would be a testimonial to an increasing opulence. A merchant's balance sheet provided a diagram for the national economy.

The mercantile system had no clean-cut expression. In England it lay embodied in a multitude of statutes and in a veritable tangle of usages which had grown up about them. A trumpeter from France might proclaim a faith in the complete efficacy of the system, and exclaim, "Let us decree a solemn Navigation Act and the isle of shopkeepers will be ruined." [42] But in far more realistic terms the Governor and Council of Virginia might with obdurate resistance solemnly resolve rather to "study to serve their own ends than his Majesty's commands." [43] To the patriotic trader, and to the law, it was evident that an importation of such commodities as vinegar, brandy, linen, leather, silk, salt, or paper from France was "a common nuisance" which cried aloud to be abated. But the folk were tolerant of "brandy for the parson, 'baccy for the clerk, laces for a lady, letters for a spy." Human frailty as well as the revenue acts demanded to be served. The commerce of a people could not be bound to the severities of a code.

The rigid lines of the statutes had to be mitigated by

an organized system of smuggling. A dealing in contra-
band goods came to be alike a respectable calling and a
national necessity. At times the revenue officers displayed
the vigilance which formal respect for the law demanded. But in general they were disposed to view with
sympathy the social function performed by "the gentlemen." [44] So the majesty of Acts of Parliament were
graciously compromised into a system of "protection,"
and the heavy duties were graduated into private assessments which a going traffic could easily bear. A system
of licenses granted to privileged persons other perquisites; and even the state was disposed to help along
honest smuggling intended to find foreign markets for
its own forbidden wares.[45] An occasional offender un-
lucky enough to be caught was a scapegoat who atoned
in his own punishment for a multitude of offenses against
the law. Thus severities were mitigated; and a policy
which on paper appeared to be "a commercial blockade"
of foreign nations, was in practice tolerant of a reasonable exchange of the wares of trade.[46] The language of
a host of statutes is not a public policy in operation; the
reality of mercantilism lies in the network of usages,
informal as well as legal, which made of it a going
system.

As a colonial policy—where the Fathers met it at first
hand—"the commercial system" was the instrument of a
rising nationalism. At first the function of the colony
was to discover, exploit, and send home the precious

metals. As this hope vanished it became the office of "the plantation" to produce staples which, at a profit to the mother country, could be refashioned into wares of trade. In time the great objective of colonial policy came to be the creation of a self-sufficient economy as broad as the empire which was coming to be. As yet England was under rather than overpopulated; its goal was rather a man-power comparable with France than breathing space for "surplus workers overseas." [47] Its interest was far more in the West Indies and the southern plantations, whose products would round out the imperial economy, than in New England, where settlement rested upon a schism within the Church, and was a threat to its trade.

In the fashion of their age statesmen looked to Nature for the broad outline of the colonial system. But in a competitive world the art of politics must modify and enforce the decrees of resource and climate. The use of such devices as duties, prohibitions of trade, and navigation acts to exclude the foreigner was only the negative part of the policy. Its positive side was a series of measures designed to lock the metropolis and the dominions together in a territorial division of labor. In the fabrication of wares England was to follow her natural bent; and each of the Colonies, in accordance with the tasks which Nature and Parliament had decreed for it, was to make the most of its distinctive advantages.

So, in a variety of acts and ordinances, "one great commercial domain" which was to be all-British was

created. In this great economy, New England was free
to build ships, even if the enterprise took away orders
from the home country. A noble experiment of the
Stuarts was designed to seduce Virginia from the cultivation of the noxious weed. But the allurements of
staples of greater moral worth did not prove enticing,
and to that Colony and Bermuda was assigned the exclusive privilege of growing tobacco.[48] In like manner
exclusive concessions were made to various Colonies in
respect to the growing of various commodities. And, as
a necessary complement in policy, the people of Great
Britain were prohibited from the cultivation of tobacco
and encroachment upon colonial trading rights. In general the plan moved along orthodox lines. It aimed at
securing to England a monopoly of manufacturing, establishing a market for the wares in the plantations, and
allowing the colonies to send raw materials in return.[49]

In the Eighteenth Century trade followed the flag. If
there was to be an exclusive market for English wares,
England must have sole dominion. The economy had to
have its armored defense; and instruments were designed
alike for military and mercantile use. A commercial
ship, with the addition of a few cannons and an extra
crew, became a man-of-war; and a merchant marine—at
once a means to foreign treasure and an instrument of
national defense—was rightly a ward of the state. The
policy could be enforced and the system maintained only
by a strong naval power; a relentless logic compelled a

navigation act designed to foster a strong mercantile
fleet. With the line between trade and war still blurred,
such vessels, as privateers and raiders, could trade with
the enemy or sever its streams of commerce. The success
of arms demanded a national self-sufficiency. A number
of trades indispensable to high national purpose—sail-
making, naval stores, gunpowder, iron mongering, mu-
nition-making—had to be fostered in the interest of the
higher national purpose. In the grand adventure the
fortunes of commerce and of empire were inseparable.[50]

Against an infinitude of detail the lines of the commercial system appear in sharp relief. In an age of intense
competition between nations, mercantilism is a word for
all that was public policy. A dynamic group interest,
chiseled into loose grooves by politics, shaped the imperial economy. The state was the active agent in a crude
system of national planning. In domestic polity its authority extended over manor, trades, traffic, manufacture, and town; it attempted to break down barriers,
to subordinate local controls, and to weave economic
activities into a national commercial fabric. In foreign
policy its aim was an exclusion of alien nations, a monopoly of wealth overseas, a fostering of colonial possessions, and the fabrication of an imperial economy. If, in
the interest of the mercantile nation, restraints were laid
upon the colonies, like restrictions were imposed upon
the once independent local authorities, and to the same
end. The state used a public policy, at home and abroad,

to round out, order, and maintain an autonomy whose political and economic boundaries were identical.[51]

The system was thus an admixture of old and new. Its tradition lay in the idea of authority and in the theory of regulation. Its novelty appears in the concept of the national economic unit and of the state as its directing agent. The regulation of commerce, as the domain of public policy, and the subordination of the pursuit of gain to public ends were alike accepted notions. It was the crown, the nation, the state, the empire which usurped the place of commune and church to claim allegiance and to direct affairs. A lingering ideology and an established regime were applied under national auspices. One facet of policy was a division of labor between parts of the empire; a second was the encouragement and regulation of manufactures; and a third was the supervision of trade to the profit of the king, the renown of the nation, and the glory of God.

Thus commerce was the commercial system. It caught up trade and traffic, comprehended manufacture within its scope, and even reached out to include the staples. And mercantilism was the policy for the commercial system. It was the law of an economic order, single and organic, at one with the political state. And over commerce the authority of Crown and Parliament was supreme.

5. *The Vitality of Mercantilism*

It is idle to attempt a judgment upon the wisdom or folly of mercantilism. In the centuries which went into its making, its adventitious creators had to take account of current circumstances in meeting the passing problems of their times. The "system" was a developing series of expediencies; its doctrines lay implicit in its policies. Its basic ideas were as unquestionable in the Eighteenth Century as the doctrine of just price had been in the Fourteenth Century and the canons of *laissez-faire* were to become in the Nineteenth Century.

What men of affairs did appeared reasonable to them. They were much too busy to contrive an elaborate apology for the intellectual commitments that lay back of their practical judgments. At most only the specific points told off in a parliamentary debate, or the studied pamphlets provoked by passing problem or occasion, can be cited in its verbal defense. The mercantilists thought and acted—or acted and thought—in response to the impact of the tiny segment of the course of human events which they encountered. The system is an abstraction —an epitome in the most general terms of a never-resting policy.

It is accordingly futile to array logic against mercantilism, or to call its doctrines to account at the bar of reason. It was to the critics of another age—rather than

to its pragmatic architects—an articulate entity, with
trim lines, a definite goal, and a philosophy. It was once
popular with later schoolmen to make of the miscellany
of practices a body of principles, to set down its departures from the norms of an orthodox political economy as "fallacies," [52] and in the manner of theology to
decry the heresy. Yet the standards for economic behavior, by which the errors of mercantilism are con-
demned, are themselves fashioned out of contemporary
idea and circumstance. From its vantage point posterity
always has a later word. But the prevailing trend in
opinion towards the necessity of control may reverse
the decree of *laissez-faire* on mercantilism. For until
truth becomes eternal and reason is timeless there can be
no final judgment.

It was, however, the pinching of the system, not its
general outline, which provoked the eighteenth-century
opposition. As is usual with policies, the-mercantilism-
that-was-to-have-been was never realized. Local usage
and group urge proved adamant to assimilation within
the larger economy. The colonies were not content
meekly to take the places in the imperial system appointed them. The landed gentry, too strongly fortified
in the social structure to be dislodged, built in the Corn
Laws a barrier about their vested interest. The competition of nations was a hazard to sole dominion and exclusive markets; it spoiled plans for a far-flung autono-
mous economy. In time the system, compromised by

local interest, agrarian class, and foreign power, came to cramp the style of colonial trade and was one of the causes of the American Revolution.

The challenge to public policy came alike at home and from the colonies. A few intellectuals had timidly begun to question the soundness of its underlying philosophy. The glorious Revolution of 1688, which for the good of the nation had dispatched the last of the House of Stuart, assigned to Parliament the place of Prince. John Locke and his school clothed the new dispensation with the novel sanctions of Nature. In the century following instances are not lacking of attacks upon specific types of regulation which enjoyed the prestige of hoary antiquity. Dean Tucker attacked the regulation of wages as "absurd and preposterous"; for "if either the journeyman will not sell his labour at the fixed or statuable price, or the master will not give it, of what use are a thousand regulating laws?" But such scattered instances were for the most part specific complaint; and it was not until Waterloo brought an interlude to national strife that *laissez-faire* began to be an articulate body of logical doctrines.[53]

In 1776, however, appeared the economic complement to the Declaration of Independence. In a treatise which bore the rather sensational title of *An Inquiry into the Nature and Causes of the Wealth of Nations*, a Scottish philosopher named Adam Smith set down in general terms what others were vaguely feeling. As a former customs official he had had practical contact with the policy; and was able to support, with a host of concrete illustrations, an argument which converted shortcoming and complaint into a general discussion of policy.[54]

Under the term commerce, Adam Smith expounds the virtues—but mostly by the vices—of the mercantile system. In a specific inquiry into "the different progress of opulence in different ages and nations," he contrasts rival policies of state. The one is "the system of commerce, the other that of agriculture." The former "is the modern system, and is best understood in our own country and our own times." [55] This division, in strict accord with the usages of his day, is not a clean-cut resolution of all activities which promote the wealth of nations into commerce and agriculture. Rather it is a contrast between the medieval or agricultural and the modern or commercial regime as rival economies for a people. In reality his abstract terms are symbols for the landed and the trading interest.[56]

He never sharpens the lines of the antithesis; and both interests are accorded roles in the productive economy. The ancient regime had its place—if a mean and narrow one—for traffic, and in commercial policy agriculture is employed to serve mercantile ends. In fact, the system of commerce then current comprehended all activities— such as trade, manufacture, and even agriculture—which produced goods or fashioned wares for the market. He is a harsh critic of much of the industrial regulation of the times; but condones the navigation acts for political reasons. He bases a dislike of particular measures not upon the esoteric ground of a lack of conformity to an orthodox theory, but because he regarded them as not conducive to the advantage of the nation. He applies to commerce notions not unlike those of the Physiocrats, lays to with a will against the strictures of mercantilism, and suggests that foreign trade be permitted to find its own natural routes. It is a valiant indictment of mercantilism; it is, save by the grace of a later philosophy, no theoretical defense of *laissez-faire*.[57]

No such probing about foundations marks the opposition of men of affairs. The attitude of Americans "in the trade" was practical. Their concern was with their material interests; their eyes were upon measures in terms of incidence upon personal fortune; their outcries were directed against threats that were immediate and tangible. The colonial merchants protested the tea tax, the molasses act, the navigation laws; they felt keenly enough to join the movement for independence. They wanted statutes to be amended or replaced by others which better reflected their opportunities for money-making. Nor, in authority themselves, would they hesitate to use the government as an instrument for the realization of a more acceptable scheme of mercantilism.[58] A freer trade with particular countries, which was diplomatically talked abroad during the Revolution, was a bait intended to secure foreign alliance.[59]

Moreover, the patriots who fought Great Britain habitually engaged in price-fixing; and among the most vehement in denunciation of regraters, forestallers, and engrossers was the Father of his Country.[60] Yet the words and acts of moneyed men are barren of criticism of the government as an agency of regulation; and even Adam Smith, who saw further ahead than any of his contemporaries, still belonged to his century and argued for no abdication of its office of overlord by the state. It was a later age which, through the darkened glass of a rising individualism, has read a general acceptance of an ex post facto *laissez-faire* into his classic lines.[61] A protest against measures which pinched was attended by an uncritical faith in the rightfulness of public control.

Nor was the voice of a rising democracy a challenge to authority. To Mr. Thomas Jefferson "those who labor upon the earth are the chosen people of God whose breasts He has made His peculiar deposit for substantial and genuine virtues." The cultivation of the soil, with its multifarious demands upon the individual, promotes independence, judgment, self-reliance, a look ahead—the very qualities which give to the rural American the qualifications for membership in a democracy. On the contrary, those who toil for others in factories and mills are reduced to a condition where "dependence begets subservience and venality suffocates the germs of virtue." So long as there is land for labor, "let us never wish to see our citizens occupied at a work bench or twirling a distaff." It is far better to "let our workshops remain in Europe" and "carry materials and provisions to workmen there" than to bring the shops and their minions over here "and with them their manners and principles." This country is no place for "starved and rickety paupers and dwarfs." Nor can Americans escape corruption if they are "piled upon one another in great cities" which like "cankers will rot out" the heart of our institutions.[62]

And Dr. Benjamin Franklin concurred. He had seen the wretched conditions of the industrious poor in the English cities; he knew that in a world market a nation's manufactures could be successful only if they depended upon pauper labor. He was as apprehensive as his neighbor from Virginia of a national policy which might develop a debauched city-dwelling population. "Manufactures," he notes, "are founded in poverty." It is "the poor without land" who "must work for others at low wages or starve that enables undertakers to carry on a manufacture." But no man, he insists, who has "a piece of land of his own, sufficient by his labor to subsist his family in plenty, is poor enough to be a manufacturer, and work for a master." And hence, so long as "there is land enough in America for our people, there can never be manufactures to any amount or values." [63]

It was apparent to Jefferson and to Franklin that they could not quite have their own way. "Our people have a decided taste for navigation and commerce" which they take from the mother country. "The servants of America are not free to follow" an engaging ideal. The way of reason might well be "to throw open the doors of commerce, to knock off all its shackles," and to give freedom to "all the vents of trade." But other countries left to America no other course than to "properly manage" our commerce to make of it an "instrument for obliging the interested nations of Europe to treat us with justice. But let us, so far as we can, use rather than make the wares of trade." The division of labor between Europe and America, which Jefferson suggests, follows the mercantile lines of the old colonial system, and public policy is an instrument in shaping such an economy. Europe might have its factories, its paupers, its corrupt body politic; husbandry and labor were the hope of the new republic.[64]

In all such protests the line of thought is clear. Americans of a democratical persuasion were champions of the domestic economy of self-sufficiency; they found the country more conducive to the pursuit of happiness than the town; they regarded the landed yeoman as the bulwark of the state. The city and the factory degraded human personality; they rendered the men they employed unfit to be citizens in such a commonwealth as it was hoped the united States were destined to become. Here there is no rebellion against the state, no outcry against regulation, no proclamation of a let-alone policy. The sturdy farmer, with little help from political overlords, was able to manage his acres, family, and miniature economy. A regime of trade was to be avoided which exacted human sacrifice and demanded the ever-watchful eye of the state. The opposition was not to mercantilism, but to the commercial economy, for which it was alike plan and policy.

Thus prevailing policy was under attack by philosopher, merchant, and democrat. Yet a discussion, little touched by abstraction, moved consistently upon the high level of expediency. It was the concrete policies—or even the money economy itself—which were under attack, not the general power of the state to prosecute them. Its specific measures were praised or blamed; but the policy of shaping an economy to national ends was universally practiced. Mercantilism was to the men of the times rather a collection of precepts for policy than a system of principles, and these were far too self-evident to the interested parties to require justification or even explicit foundation. A state must, for purposes of offense and defense, stand among the nations of the world as a self-sufficient economic entity. It must, among its domestic and colonial possessions, foster the production of a food supply and of all wares instrumental to war. Its shipping, for success at sea and to the glory of the realm, must be developed to the limit of the nation's capacity. Its internal activities must be subdued by rule to the public good. Its foreign trade, through appropriate measures, must be shaped into a great source of new wealth.

The drama of trade "with parts overseas" appealed to the imagination. It threw the more prosaic role of the domestic system into the shadows. From the romantic ends of the world raw materials and half-fabricated products came to London and went away again enhanced with the value added by manufacture. The wares of trade were made to pass through the narrow arteries of the metropolis where the state might from the passing traffic exact its rightful due. It was the touch from overseas which was transforming an agrarian into a commercial economy, impelling England to emerge from its rustic retreat and allowing the nation of shopkeepers to vie with Spain, Holland, and France for the mastery of the seas.

Against all the glamor of the times commerce as word, aspiration, and high adventure came into the ascendancy. All through the century and long before it was pregnant with new life. The word was to the Fathers an epitome of the great movement which was transforming the ancient regime into the mercantile world. Its far-sweeping domain was not to be hemmed in by a logician's rigid lines of inclusion and exclusion. In the sundry statutes concerned with trade regulation and navigation, and their ramification into every nook and corner of commercial life, a national system for the strict regulation of all economic activity stands revealed. The revolu-

tionary process which in a few short years converted
colonials into Americans did not seriously disturb the
mercantile cast of mind.

At the time of the Revolution the colonists accepted
the doctrines and maxims of mercantilism. They even
admitted many of the regulations of the old colonial
system to be good—because they could not think of
plausible alternatives. They were insistent in attacks
upon measures; they were quick to defend their own
rights; they were resourceful in distinguishing between
"internal" and "external" taxes and in setting off duties
for revenue from the regulation of trade.[65] But, in all
the display of dialectic inspired by the patriotic cause,[66]
there is no departure from the political economy which
was current.[67] The abstract power of the state to shape
commerce to the service of the commonwealth remains
unquestioned.[68]

A touch of the eternal clings to mercantilism. It has
had its enduring values. It was temporarily abandoned
by England only when the nation had become supreme
in manufacturing and a far-flung imperial economy had
been attained. It was given up because a freer trade
would better serve the imperial cause and promote the
mercantilist ends. In the United States the trend has
taken its own course. In domestic policy mercantilism
has made way for a qualified *laissez-faire*, which has
come under attack because of a lack of harmony between performance and promise. In foreign policy, save

for a period preceding the Civil War, it has retained its eminence.

As the decades of the Twentieth Century pass, a neo-mercantilism is in the making. A policy of competitive nationalism, adapted to the exigencies of the industrial state, is staging a comeback. Where *laissez-faire* lingers, it is justified as an instrument of national wealth. The argument is that it will—more surely than any program of regulation—promote trade, encourage manufacture, and advance the liberal arts. *Laissez-faire* is today furbished out with the apologetic trappings of an older mercantilism. If matters of common concern are to be left alone by the state, it is because the wealth of the nation—rechristened prosperity—is presumed to lie that way.

· V ·

A Debate Among
Mercantilists

1. *Attitudes and Interests*

THE CONVENTION of 1787—to the comfort of jurists
and the joy of scholars—did not write a gloss to its own
text. It met in executive session; and whatever minutes
were necessary from day to day were eventually de-
stroyed. The journals of some five of its members present the greater part of what we know about what was
thought, said, and done behind closed doors, from which
was presently to emerge an instrument of national government. Yates and Lansing[1] scribbled their own notes
upon—and reactions to—the proceedings; but neither
liked the course events were taking, and in disgust at
the trend toward nationalism left the city long before
the end. Madison's journal was no static affair; he repeatedly allowed his personal remembrance to freshen
his entries; and it is not surprising that his gradual swing
to anti-federalism—the product of the exigencies of a

long life in politics—came to be sanctioned in his record of the Convention.[2]

The notes of McHenry and of Paterson are mere fragments, usefui as corroborative evidence, but adding little not otherwise known. The memoirs and biographies of the members, written many years later and usually by other hands, do not escape an endowment of meaning—usually quite unconscious—from the events, the issues, and the commitments of another age.[3] And the expository literature of the day—one degree removed, such as the miscellany of leaflets which make up *The Federalist*—were intended to make the document seem reasonable to men disposed to discover hidden away with its clauses political fallacies to be avoided or national dangers too great to be endured.

All in all the evidence is less than we should like. A transcript of proceedings and an official gloss on the text would serve every need. But the sum of relevant material is far in excess of the body of documents from which skilled historians have constructed the culture of many a by-gone era. It is the importation of meaning, opinion, and intellectual procedure from the alien world of here and now which makes evidence inconclusive, muddles understanding, and shunts inquiry to false leads. No multiplication in the mass of materials could overcome such a source of confusion. The formation of the Constitution was a late eighteenth-century event. The task of the delegates was to contrive a government for a union of independent states and to repair the breach in the national economy caused by separation from Great Britain. Their usage in respect to words was that of their own day; their minds, in argument, followed the prevailing paths through affairs of state. The evidence of the debates—in its setting of word, idea, and occasion—is adequate. If the obvious fact of its date— with its implications—be brought to inquiry, the line of debate on every major matter at issue stands out with a light and sharpness almost of certainty.

It is but a step from the open corridor of the Eighteenth Century to the secret chamber of the Convention. A thumbing of pages reveals the atmosphere of mercantilism. A spirit of nationalism—too strong for erasure—dominates the Convention. The interminable struggle of European powers, with Waterloo still nearly three decades in the future, was a series of national trade wars. A nominal peace, as the former colonials had discovered, was only "a state of undeclared hostility." [4] The united States might, as they were a little later advised, beware of foreign alliances; but they could not put their affairs beyond the reach of the vindictive policies of rival nations. The delegates were, in general, America-conscious; and among some of them appears a spirit of belligerency astonishing in its vehemence. There was fear that "foreign powers" would try to "intermeddle in our affairs, and spare no expense to influence them." Such, according to Mr. Elbridge Gerry, was the prevailing thought in Massachusetts. Mr. Mason of Virginia agreed; the National Legislature should be "restrained to Natives." There was a real danger that foreign spies would seek to "work themselves into our Councils" and give "a pernicious turn" to our affairs, "particularly our commercial regulations," especially since "the great House of British Merchants will spare no pains to insinuate the instruments of their views into the Government." [5]

The fear of alien dominance—especially in the domain of commercial policy—was not easily allayed. A number of the delegates had been foreign-born and foreigners had given loyal service in the Revolution. Yet many of the members seemed to feel that "for commercial reasons" aliens in Congress would be a danger. Mr. Morris [6] had no objection to immigration, but did not trust aliens as legislators. In particular he did not wish to see in our public Councils "those philosophical gentlemen, those citizens of the world as they call themselves." [7] He would not trust them. "The men who can shake off their attachments to their own country can never love any other. These attachments are the wholesome prejudices which uphold all Governments." Admit a Frenchman into the Congress "and he will study to increase the commerce of France"; an Englishman will feel an "equal biass" in favor of that of England.

In the end those that would safeguard and insulate the new system against the "pernicious" influences of the competitive nationalist states of Europe gained their point. In spite of the pleas for liberality by Franklin and Madison, in spite of the catalogue of foreign heroes serving during the Revolution, in spite of warnings from Wilson that it would discourage emigration of "meritorious" individuals,[8] the Convention voted to lengthen residence requirements for Senators from four to nine years. They refused to lower the seven-year requirement for the House and voted down an amendment that would have exempted immigrant foreigners who were already citizens. They refused to be "polite at the expence of prudence"; those who would wield the power they were granting must have demonstrated American loyalty during a long period of probation.

The same note appears in an all but Marxian pitting of interest against interest in the state. Mr. Pinckney of South Carolina resolved "the people of the United States" into "three classes": (1) *"Professional men* who must from their particular pursuits always have a considerable weight in the Government"; (2) *"Commercial men,* who may or may not have weight, as a wise or injudicious policy is pursued"; and (3) "the *landed interest,* the owners, and cultivators of the soil." He declared that even under a "wise" commercial policy "the merchant will not or ought not for a considerable time to have much weight in the political scale," and that the landed interest "are and ought ever to be the governing spring in the system." [9]

The landed interest, he felt, required no artificial help from the government. It was destined to prevail because of its importance, the weight of its numbers, and a foolish policy in respect to trade. "In commercial policy," he insisted, "we have unwisely considered ourselves as the inhabitants of an old instead of a new country" and "have adopted the maxims of a State full of people and manufactures and established in credit." [10] In disregard of "our true interest" and "the future importance of our commerce" we have "rashly and prematurely engaged in schemes as extensive as they are imprudent." A touch of scorn attends his declaration that nothing is to be feared from a national solicitude for the mercantile interest. As a true American, he declared that no "nobility" can "spring from commerce." [11]

The same note is sounded time and again. In the debate over the method of electing Senators, Elbridge Gerry urged choice by the state legislatures for the protection of the "commercial and monied interest." In reply James Wilson of Pennsylvania questioned whether such a bulwark was secure since it "was now complained" that the state legislatures "sacrificed the commercial to the landed interest." [12] And Alexander Hamilton, translating interests into objects of policy, could with a quiet equanimity contemplate the extinction of state lines and argue that the separate commonwealths "are not necessary for any of the great purposes of commerce, revenue, or agriculture." [13]

It is Madison, however, who is most sensitive to the detail of interests which make up the state. Within the first week of real work he reminds his colleagues that "all civilized Societies" are "divided into different Sects, Factions and Interests," as they happen "to consist of rich and poor, debtors and creditors, the landed, the manufacturing," and "the commercial interests." [14] At a later stage of the proceedings, he insists upon a division of "people" into "classes having a real or supposed difference of interests." He instances, almost as before, "creditors and debtors, farmers, merchants and manufacturers,[15] and particularly the distinction of rich and poor." [16] Here Madison, in a mild alarm, is pointing out factions which will disturb the unity and harmony of the body politic. The differences in interest between farmers, manufacturers, and merchants are superficial; the real clash lies between the "have's" and the "have not's." [17]

A statement in the debate over membership in the House of Representatives is of like import. A property qualification for suffrage had been proposed as an insurance of stability and conservatism. Mr. King had objected that "there might be great danger in requiring landed property as a qualification since it would exclude the monied interest." [18] Mr. Madison heartily concurred. He stated that "every class of citizens should

have an opportunity of making their rights be felt and
understood"; divided citizens into "the landed, the commercial, and the manufacturing"; and insisted that although the last "bear as yet a small proportion to the
first," their interests should not be left "to the care and
the impartiality" of the agrarian group.[19] The special
mention of manufacturing is, of course, not its distinction from commerce. On the contrary, its specification
is to enhance its prospective importance to the nation.
Here, as elsewhere, Madison indulges no argument for
a limitation of the powers of Congress.

These gentlemen—Pinckney, Gerry, Wilson, Hamilton, Madison—were representatives of commonwealths
as diverse as South Carolina, Massachusetts, Pennsylvania, New York, and Virginia. They differed greatly
in the opinions as to sound commercial policy.[20] Yet
they were as one in giving a broad sweep to commerce
and in viewing their task as the resolution of a conflict
of interests into an orderly state.[21]

Nor does even the question of popular habits of
spending—the very epitome of mercantilism—escape the
debates. The people of the Eighteenth Century, forsak-
ing the austere values of the Middle Ages, had become
tolerant of luxury and even of extravagant expenditure.
But, as staunch nationalists, the older moral prohibition
had been subdued into the provisos that indulgence
should be limited to wares of native origin and that indolence and display were not to be encouraged among

laborers. The use, however sumptuous, of domestic
articles, served to promote agriculture, encourage manufacture, stimulate trade, and give employment to workers. But the consumption of costly wares from overseas
was a threat to the economy of the realm. Any loss of
specie in itself was deplorable, but that a foreign nation
through sale of manufactures should reap the resulting
gains was tainted with treason. By the maxims of the
times such a course, if long continued, would be equivalent to political suicide. Members of the Convention
were not ignorant of so sound a principle of political
economy. So Mr. Mason moved that the Congress be
given the power "to·enact sumptuary laws," and in support presented an elaborate argument.

He insisted that "no government can be maintained
unless the manners be made consonant to it." So important an end was not to be left to indirection. Although
"a proper regulation of excises and of trade may do a
great deal," it is "best to have an express provision."
The objection that sumptuary laws "were contrary to
nature" was "a vulgar error"; their very purpose was,
not "to extinguish," but to give "proper direction" to
"the love of distinction." Ellsworth objected to the direct attack on the problem. "The best remedy" was "to
enforce taxes and debts"; and, so far as "the regulation
of eating and drinking can be reasonable, it is provided
for in the power of taxation." Elbridge Gerry closed

the discussion by remarking that "the law of necessity is the best sumptuary law." [22]

Only three states—Delaware, Maryland, and Georgia —were willing to include a specific enactment: the others seem to have felt that the potential authority should spring from the tax clause and that "necessity" could be served best by its regulatory use. [23]

The motion was lost, but its objective was not questioned. It was still accepted that by their clothes ye shall know them. The trappings of station and rank were still to proclaim the mercantilist state.

2. *The Concern over Commerce*

A concern over commerce was native to such a gathering; its efforts were to be directed towards a sound commercial policy. But policy must wait upon a grant of power, and power was to be entrusted only to an authority capable of its exercise.

In the Convention itself the word "commerce" was frequently upon the lips of the members. It was a subject of consideration, a stake in the government, an interest to be conserved whatever the political topic under consideration. As a member of the Virginia delegation, Madison had helped Edmund Randolph draft the speech with which the Convention was opened. In his notes he records in an abbreviated form a list of "the many advantages" which Randolph stated the United

States ought to acquire, but which "were not obtainable under the Confederation." Its particulars are "a productive impost—counteraction of the commercial regulation of other nations—pushing of commerce *ad libitum*," and a generous pair of "etc.'s." [24] A "pushing" of commerce "at will, as much as one pleases," is intriguing in its implications.

Madison, familiar with the speech as a fellow-author, is content to let it pass at that. But luckily, McHenry, hearing it for the first time, resolves the brief Latin tag into a bill of particulars. Specifically, as he reports, Randolph declared that the present Union was unable "to produce certain blessings." Among them are the five per cent impost; control of the paper money evil and other "benefits of which we are singly incapable." This positive action, encompassed in Madison's abbreviated phrase, includes "establishment of great national works —the improvement of inland navigation—agriculture—manufactures—a freer intercourse among the citizens." [25] It would be hard to crowd into a shorter space more of the essence of the national state. Commerce is the orbit of a national economic policy.

A consciousness—a concern for the commercial interest—threads its way through the debates. It appears as a constant attendant to the recurrent sectional issue; it flames when a regulation of trade affects the plantations of the South. A clause was put forward forbidding Congress to levy a tax on the importation of slaves. In

opposition Mr. Luther Martin of Maryland contended
that the slave trade was "inconsistent with the principles
of the revolution and dishonorable to the American
character." [26] His counter-proposal that Congress be
allowed "a prohibition or tax on the importation of
slaves," assumed that the power to tax is the power to
prohibit. His insistence upon power in the general government to abolish the traffic in negroes found vocal
support among delegates from states as far south as Virginia. It was soon clear that all the examples adduced
from "Greece, Rome, and other antient States" and the
sanction of Holy Writ would never convince a majority
of the members that the slave trade was anything but
despicable; the overwhelming sentiment of the Convention was for abolition of it.

The delegates from Georgia and the Carolinas, mindful of maxims of strategy for the defense, launched a
counter-attack. Pinckney, as self-appointed leader of the
minority group, succeeded in linking the prohibition of
"black cargo" with the requirement of a two-thirds vote
of Congress to pass any commercial regulation. There
were immediate murmurs from the New England con-
tingent. Gorham of Massachusetts did not see the
"propriety" of the maneuver. He desired it to be remembered that "the Eastern States had no motive to
Union but a commercial one." [27] But Pinckney, seeing
the opposition in confusion, pressed his advantage. The
two clauses were referred to committee.

There a compromise was quickly reached and the issue amicably settled. The clause setting a maximum duty of ten dollars per slave for twenty years—after which the traffic should cease—was passed without opposition; [28] and when the provision in regard to commercial regulation again reached the floor, the alignment had shifted. Mason still felt that a two-thirds majority should be required. Otherwise the Southern States, a minority in both Houses, "will deliver themselves bound hand and foot to the Eastern States." [29] But the South Carolinians, honorable bargainers, paid their score. General Pinckney confessed "that he had himself . . . prejudices against the Eastern States before he came here" but that he had found their representatives "as liberal and candid as any men whatever." "It was the true interest of the Southern States to have no regulation of commerce." In consideration, however, of "the loss brought on the commerce of the Eastern States by the revolution," and in return for "their liberal conduct towards the views of South Carolina," he thought that "no fetters should be imposed on the power of making commercial regulations." [30]

In the issue of the moment, future as well as current interests were at stake. In the rising American economy the position of New England needed to be firmly established. The compromise was a guarantee that a navigation act would be passed, restricting American trade to American bottoms, and thus giving a "spring" to East-

ern shipping. It would raise freights, undoubtedly, and
"bear hard" a little while on the South, but in return
the staple-producing states would gain in "the general
security afforded by the increase of our maritime
strength." [31]

The result was to be to the mutual advantage of all
sections. The South alone faced the prospect of loss;
for the encouragement of Northern manufactures it had
to surrender the power to block the regulation of trade.
But in consequence a sectional division of labor would
allow all the members of the Union to exploit to the
full their peculiar advantages. The Eastern States would
attain a position which could never have been theirs in
the old colonial system. But "what enriches a part enriches the whole"; [32] under the guidance of a national
council, the clashing interests would be subdued to a
national good. And as members of "a great empire," the
United States would be able to pursue a commercial
policy in the international sphere. [33]

In like manner the power of commerce needed to be
strengthened in respect to domestic matters. There was
an insistent demand that the new system be given adequate powers to undertake a program of internal development. Pinckney, mindful of the "mistaken commercial
policy" of the impotent Confederation, proposed that
the new Congress be granted broad specific powers to
effectuate the desired end. For "the promotion of agriculture, commerce, trades and manufactures," Congress

was to be authorized to establish "public institutions" and to bestow "rewards and immunities." [34] And, again, Gouverneur Morris proposed that the Constitution provide for the setting up of a Council of State "to assist the President in conducting the Public Affairs." Assigned to a Secretary of Domestic Affairs was the duty "to attend to matters of general police, the State of Agriculture and manufactures, the opening of roads and navigations, and the facilitating communications thro' the United States." [35] Such necessities were not disputed, nor were the proposals debated. They were sent along, with others of their kind, to the Committee of Detail.

So, too, with the proposition that corporations be created by Act of Congress. To the Crown such a power had been a great source of revenue. It had been customary to issue exclusive privileges for the importation and sale, or the making and vending, of important wares, and such monopolies had come to be commonly regarded as nuisances. The question arose when Mr. Madison, looking to the establishment of canal and turnpike companies, moved that Congress be empowered "to grant charters of incorporation." [36] Rufus King objected; it was a dangerous clause since it would assuredly stir up opposition against ratification. Some will fear the establishment of a bank; to others it will imply "mercantile monopolies." But Wilson did not think the argument valid. It would prove a most beneficial clause, and as to authority to create mercantile monopolies, it was "already included in the power to regulate trade." Mr. Mason, avowing that "he was afraid of monopolies of every sort," begged to differ. They were not implied by any part of the Constitution as he saw it; Mr. Wilson must be mistaken.[37]

Madison's motion was lost; but Wilson's remark continued to plague Mason. For when the time came for the delegates to put pen to parchment, Mason steadfastly refused. Instead he elaborately drew up on the back of his printed copy of the new instrument his carefully considered "objections to this Constitution of Government." And among them was written "the Congress may grant monopolies in trade and commerce." [38] The wisdom of a grant of power containing so great a hazard might be questioned. But that such an authority lay within the power to regulate commerce no one disputed.

Its punitive character and its importance to trade combine to make bankruptcy [39] a matter of consequence. Its incidence upon the economic activities of the country had been brought home to the members through the prevailing depression. The matter, however, did not engage the delegates until late in the session.

On August 29th the clause stating that "full faith shall be given in each State to the acts of the Legislatures . . . and judicial proceedings of every other State" was offered for discussion. Mr. Williamson of North Carolina wanted to know what it meant; and Mr. Wilson, a member of the drafting committee, explained that "a judgment in one State should be the ground of actions in other States, and that acts of the Legislatures should be included, for the sake of Acts of insolvency." [40] At this point Mr. Pinckney, desiring to make the implication explicit, moved that power be granted to the Congress "to establish uniform laws upon the subject of bankruptcies." The motion passed without opposition and was referred to a committee for phrasing.

When, five days later, the revised clause was reported out for a vote, Sherman objected. "Bankruptcies were in some cases punishable with death by the laws of England—he did not chuse to grant a power by which that might be done here." [41] Gouverneur Morris scoffed at the possibility. Bankruptcy was "an extensive and delicate subject," a national uniformity was needed in its regulation, and there was "no danger of abuse of the power by the Legislature of the United States." When the vote was called for, the count was nine states in favor, one state alone—Connecticut—in dissent. Thus authority over the institution through which commerce liquidates its unprofitable ventures was quickly and effectively transferred to the general government. [42]

Thus in issue, incident, and implication the concern over commerce runs throughout the debates. Concrete proposals invite difference of opinion. Although detail may be avoided, there is no unanimity as to the concretions which are to be set down in the document. Yet

there is everywhere in evidence an intent to endow the
general government with the power to formulate a
policy for the national economy, a power which is to
extend to trade, manufactures, the staples of agriculture, internal improvements, and the creation of corporations. A broad grant of power was to be given to
Congress in a clean-cut clause of utmost brevity. If possible a single key word must here—as elsewhere in the
Constitution—be made to tell the story.[43] It was of no
avail to bother with manufacture or production; words
of such narrow confine, even if set down in clusters,
could only have made up an irregular verbal fragment.
A more comprehensive term—such as business or industry—was not for many decades to become available.
The choice was narrowed to traffic, trade, and commerce. Traffic would not do; it was lowly in origin and
clearly headed for vulgar verbal company. Trade was
too specialized in meaning and too barren in larger implications to serve the occasion.[44] Commerce excelled in
the larger breadth and range, the greater dignity and
prestige which attached to it. And commerce alone had
competency for so high a verbal duty.

Nor were the actualities of commerce boxed within a
verbal category. On the contrary the delegates selected
from all the offerings of the language the word which
marked out the most inclusive range of activities. It had
to do triple duty for dealings "with foreign nations,
among the several States, and with the Indian Tribes."

The three provinces are distinct; they are domains for different types of regulation; they are invitations to distinct ventures into public policy; yet the commerce of the Constitution comprehends them all. A control of Indian affairs might have been set down as a separate item; or it might have been rested upon treaty-making. At one time it was in danger of being drawn under the war power, and it was a later addendum to the commerce clause. The regulation is far broader than anything the people of the times meant by traffic. It comprehends such correspondence as is carried on with hymn-books, sermons, tomahawks, and gunpowder.[45] Back of it lies a long chapter in the clash of cultures along a retreating but omnipresent frontier.[46] In its relation to the Indians the key word can mean nothing short of association or intercourse. But the word which must have breadth to assure a national control over Indian affairs, is used to designate the domains "with foreign affairs" and "among the several States" over which the regulatory power of Congress was to extend. The ease with which it could be accommodated to such a trio of national purposes attests the catholic character of commerce.

3. *Taxation as Regulation*

Authority over commerce was to the Fathers no single grant of power. A political dominion over the eco-

nomic activities of the country was to be achieved by
the use of techniques of control, all well known to the
current art of politics. Among such usages of commercial regulation the device of taxation and the control
over imports and exports were of the first importance.

The proposal to endow the federal legislature with the
power "to lay and collect taxes, imposts, and excises"
provoked little debate. It seems obvious that, before it
was proposed on the floor, its probable effects had been
thoroughly discussed *in camera* by influential delegates.
For, immediately it was reached, Mr. Mason of Virginia
insisted that it be understood from the first "that no tax
should be laid on exports." He frankly admitted that he
spoke on behalf of "the productions of the Southern, or
staple states" and hoped that they would not be denied
"this security." There was some little flurry of debate;
Madison, Wilson, and Gouverneur Morris disliked the
prohibition; but Roger Sherman thought "the matter
had been adjusted" and considered "it wrong to tax
exports except it might be such articles as ought not to
be exported." [47] The concept of the taxing power as
a regulatory measure seemed patent to all, and for the
time the Convention wasted no more words on the
matter.

Later a storm broke over the proposal to deny to
Congress authority to levy duties on exports. Its support
came largely from the southern states who would not
intrust to the general government the power to erect a

barrier between the staples which they produced and the foreign markets in which they were sold. The proposition was in strict accord with the position which the southern states had occupied in the colonial system of England. It was, as even those who opposed it admitted, an accurate reflection of the economic realities of the times. In its terms raw materials were to go abroad; they were to be paid for in tropical products and the wares of manufacture.

The opposition came from the rising manufacturing interest. It rested upon the accepted theory of mercantilism, but with the United States cast in the role formerly played by Great Britain. If an American national economy was to be rounded out, manufactures must be encouraged, and a division of labor must be effected within the states between the production of raw materials and the fabrication of finished wares. To that end a tax on exports—perhaps their prohibition in particular instances—was not out of order.[48] Here and there among the delegates, ideas lingered on from the old colonial system; it was particularly feared that the export duties on raw materials would react to the discouragement of agriculture. The opposition employed the best of mercantile doctrine accommodated to the exigencies of an ambitious new republic.

This alignment—in interest, outlook, and logic—runs through the debates. Oliver Ellsworth, in behalf of the prohibition, argued that a tax on exports would discourage industry, that uniformity in rates could not be achieved, and that "incurable jealousies" would ensue.[49] Gouverneur Morris brought to the matter the idealism of a rising manufacturing interest. He countered with the plea that "local considerations ought not to impede the general interest." He argued that "the State of the Country, also, will change, and render duties on exports," such as "skins, beaver and other peculiar raw materials, politic in the view of encouraging American Manufactures." [50] Falling back to current realities, he stated that "all countries having peculiar articles tax the exportation of them," and insisted that a tax on lumber and on livestock "would fall on the West Indies and punish their restriction on our trade." Here was a weapon of national power, for "in case of a dearth" we "may extort what we please"; and, besides—with a quick shift of subject—"taxes on exports are a necessary source of revenue." [51] Gouverneur Morris knew that the West Indies had done everything possible—even playing with treason—to keep the trade open, that lack of commerce with the states had fallen heavily upon the islands, and that fifteen thousand slaves had starved to death. Yet, in the prevailing thought, a nation could gain wealth only at the expense of another nation; and he could contemplate with equanimity the punishment of a British possession for a situation which was beyond its control. In the competitive commerce of 1787 it was war to the hilt.

In similar terms Madison objected to the prohibition. Sound—after the manner of his day—in political economy, he insisted that "we ought to be governed by national and permanent views," and that a tax on exports, "though it may not be expedient at present, may be so hereafter." It "may and probably will be necessary" for "the same purposes as the regulation of imports," namely, "for revenue—domestic manufacture—and procuring equitable regulations from other nations." [52] Wilson concurred that "to deny this power is to take from the common government half the regulation of trade." In his opinion "a power over exports might be more effectual than that over imports in obtaining beneficial treaties of commerce." Fitzsimmons was in hearty accord; although there was no immediate demand, at the "proper time" when America "should become a manufacturing Country," a tax on exports might become necessary. [53]

Not one of those who supported the prohibition questioned the use of export taxes for purposes of regulation. On the contrary their opposition proceeded from their knowledge that it would be so used. In the end vested interest proved more powerful than possible future necessity; and through the votes of Massachusetts and all the states south of Maryland "security" was voted to the staples. In like manner, although the issue did not provoke extended debate, a tax on imports was accepted as a device of regulation. [54]

Far more significant than the result is the texture of the argument. The power to tax imports and exports is a device to be used in the regulation of commerce. The power to tax—like the power to make war—is to be employed against the commercial enemy, to help along the making of treaties, to force trade concessions, and to encourage manufactures. Here is no nineteenth-century argument, no expression of a later doctrine of free trade, no gesture of peace on earth to an expectant society of nations. Instead the parade of reasons, with all their implications, attest the march of minds steeped in the politics of mercantilism. The victory for the prohibition was no triumph of a more liberal philosophy. It was the cause of the Southern planters which prevailed in the reaffirmation of the place of the staples in the older economy; the Northern members could not risk the "shipwreck of the whole" on the rock of Southern oppositon to a single clause.[55]

The discussion of imports, of exports, of taxes, always went forward in terms of established trade interests. In the Convention there was no outcry against the creation of a tyranny that might enhance the price of cloth and shoes or might force down the price of the farmer's wool.[56] The use of the taxing power to discourage imports, to speed exports to foreign markets, to encourage manufacture, to give direction to commerce was questioned by none. Names come after common sense begins to be questioned; and, although they would have raised their eyebrows at a term not yet in general use, the Fathers are mercantilists.

To the delegates commerce was a multiplex of activities to be encouraged or depressed as the wealth of the nation might demand. A mercantilist mind alone—certainly not an apostle of a nineteenth-century *laissez-faire*—could think of a control of commerce by the device of taxation as a strategy to shape an economy and to bring foreign powers to terms.

4. *The Sphere of National Authority*

A concern with concrete problems pointed in a single direction. The break with Great Britain, the rift in the economy, and the necessity of its repair were always in the minds of the delegates. A proper commercial policy demanded an adequate instrument of government equipped with all necessary and proper powers.

The sphere of national authority was easily marked out as "common defence, security of liberty, and general welfare." [57] It was set down in functional terms in a resolution presented by Mr. Randolph in the speech with which he opened the Convention. The new Congress was "to enjoy the Legislative Rights" of the Confederation "and moreover to legislate in all cases to which the separate States are incompetent or in which the harmony of the United States may be interrupted by the exercise of individual Legislation." [58] In spite of general terms, its stress and import were perfectly clear. It was accepted without a dissenting vote.[59]

The resolution came up again some six weeks later. The final vote on the composition of the Congress was taken on the morning of July 16th; in the afternoon the small states, flushed with victory in the matter of Senate representation, were not loath to return to the question of powers. As it was read, Mr. Butler, who had been willing "to go great lengths" in granting authority to the right sort of a Congress, arose to question "the extent of this power," and particularly "the word *incompetent*";[60] "the vagueness of the terms rendered it impossible for any precise judgment to be formed." To Mr. Gorham, "the vagueness of the terms" was the mark of their "propriety." The "general principles" now being established are to be "extended hereafter into details which will be precise and explicit." No further action was possible; Mr. Randolph, hoping to rally his forces, fought for postponement; the Convention adjourned for the day—probably into a number of caucuses.

At the call to business the next day the issue was resumed. Mr. Sherman believed it would be difficult to draw the line between "the powers of the General Legislatures and those to be left with the States"; and besides, "he did not like the definitions contained in the Resolution." He proposed a revised statement that the Congress "make laws binding on the people of the

United States in all cases which may concern the common interests of the Union, but not to interfere with the Government of the individual States in any matters of internal police which respect the Government of such States only, and wherein the General Welfare of the United States is not concerned." [61] On its face this was little more than an indirect statement of Randolph's resolution; but the bare mention of inviolate rights of the states as a limitation upon Congressional power was out of key. Mr. Morris pointed out that the internal police "ought often to be infringed," as "in the case of paper money and other tricks by which Citizens of other States may be affected." The Convention was in accord; and by eight states to two—Connecticut and Maryland—the Sherman substitute was rejected.

But the Convention was not yet done with the subject. Mr. Bedford, a little nettled over charges of localism against the small states, moved an amendment. He moved, outdoing Randolph, to empower the Congress "to legislate in all cases for the general interests of the Union." [62] His amendment permitted congressional action in the positive case of "the general interests" as well as in the negative ones of state incompetency and interference. For the moment it drove Randolph from his nationalistic position; he called it "a formidable idea indeed" involving "the power of violating all the laws and constitutions of the States, and of intermeddling with their police." [63] Mr. Bedford was quick in retort;

his clause was "not more extensive or formidable" than Randolph's; the national legislature must of necessity be empowered to promote the general welfare; he had effected no change in the resolution, "no State being *separately* competent to legislate for the *general interest* of the Union." On the vote Bedford's substitute was carried, six states to four. And so it was referred to the Committee of Detail as a guiding principle in selecting and enumerating power.

Here was a frame of reference. But it was, according to Mr. Madison, "a mere sketch" whose "general terms and phrases" needed "to be reduced to proper details." That task was already well under way. In addition to the Virginia plan, of which the quoted resolution was a part, Pinckney had presented an alternative trial at a constitution; and later, in the heat of the debates, Paterson had put forward, possibly for bargaining purposes, the New Jersey plan, based on "the federal principle." [64] The Pinckney plan proposed as a means of raising revenue the old quota system,[65] in effect under the Confederation, and endowed the federal government with authority to compel its payment. It entrusted to Congress—note the singular—exclusive "power of regulating Trade and levying Imposts" with the one limitation that "in Times of Scarcity" each state might lay an Embargo.[66]

The Paterson, or New Jersey, plan, worked out in elaborate detail, tended to the same general effect. Import duties were to be added to quotas as means of revenue; [67] and the Congress was to be authorized "to pass Acts for the regulation of Trade and Commerce as well with foreign Nations as with each other." [68] Enforcement was to be entrusted to "the Common Law Judiciarys" of the state in which any "offence" was committed; but an appeal "for the correction of all errors both in law and fact" lay "to the Judiciary of the United States." [69] Revenue was to be raised by customs duties. The regulation of commerce was to proceed by way of "punishments, fines, forfeitures, and penalties"— presumably of a monetary character [70]—"for contravening" acts and rules. Here, as with Randolph, the power to tax and the power to regulate are common facets of the power to govern.

All of these plans—with sundry separate resolutions— had been before under discussion for weeks. [71] They had all been critically probed by the delegates in Convention, in Committee of the Whole, in conference, and in caucuses. After a month in which a discussion of basic principles went on, enlivened by the struggle between the big and the little states for the control of the general government, resolutions were voted on, principles were accepted or rejected, agreements were reached, and on July 23rd, Mr. Elbridge Gerry moved that "the proceedings for establishing a National Government be referred to a Committee to prepare and report a Constitution conformable thereto."

The Committee of Detail [72] thus set up went to work on July 27th to whip resolutions into shape and to weld them together into a unified instrument of government. In the drafting of the Constitution the Committee resolved to employ two simple criteria.[73] The one was "to use simple and precise language according to the example of the Constitutions of the several states." The other was "to insert essential principles only, lest the operations of government should be clogged by rendering those provisions permanent and unalterable, which ought to be accommodated to times and events."

Detail after detail went into a rough draft still in need of refinement. The powers of Congress are listed with certain "exceptions and restrictions." It was agreed "to raise money by taxation unlimited as to sum, for the past and future debts and necessities of the union and to establish rules for collection." The exception was that no tax was to be laid on exports; and certain restrictions, such as uniformity in assessment and proportionality in respect to population, were appended.[74] Under the head of "restrictions" with respect to taxation are set down "to regulate commerce" and an addendum, in the hand of Rutledge, "both foreign and Domestic"; and, again in the same hand, "no state to levy a duty on Imports." A trio of exceptions trails, "No duty on exports"; "No prohibition on Importations of such inhabitants . . . as the States think proper to admit";[75] and "no duties by way of such prohibition." [76]

At about the same time another need was first re-
marked, and down the page near the war power and
the power to punish pirates Rutledge scribbled on the
margin, "Indian Affairs." In the first draft of the Constitution arranged in the now familiar form, Section 8
in Article I appears in the handwriting of James Wilson,
thus: "The Legislature of the United States shall have
the Power to lay and collect Taxes, Duties, Imposts and
Excises; to regulate Commerce"—and in an emendation
in Rutledge's handwriting, "with foreign nations and
among the several States." [77] In this form with the added
phrase, "and with the Indian tribes," it has remained. In
due course it was presented to the Convention; and an
entry in Madison's journal for August 16th prosaically
reads, "clause for regulating commerce with foreign
nations, etc., agreed to *nem. con.*" [78]

As with "the commerce clause" so with others. The
rough material submitted by delegates was through
phrasing and fitting shaped into a statement of powers.
In this process of refinement, far too intricate to be detailed here, the Convention, the Committee of Detail,
the Committee on Unfinished Parts, and the Committee
on Stile all had their parts. It was subjected to constant
scrutiny and repeated revision; and as clauses ran
through edition after edition to studied statement, it
would have been strange, indeed, if shade of meaning
and integrity of comma were absolute proof against
continuous workmanship. In the end a national au-

thority, so far as "the common defence and the general welfare would allow," was chiseled into a number of broad and overlapping grants of power.

In spite of its importance, the competence of national authority provoked little opposition. The structure of the government and the system of elections touched off far deeper feelings and promoted far more extended debate. But as soon as such structural matters were out of the way, it was easy enough to endow Congress with comprehensive powers to promote the wealth of the nation. So in lines which have become classic it was set down that "The Congress shall have Power

"To lay and collect Taxes, Duties, Imposts and Excises, to pay the Debts and provide for the common Defence and general Welfare of the United States; . . .

"To borrow Money on the credit of the United States;

"To regulate Commerce with foreign Nations, and among the several States, and with the Indian Tribes;

"To establish an uniform Rule of Naturalization, and uniform Laws on the subject of Bankruptcies throughout the United States;

"To coin Money, regulate the Value thereof, and of foreign Coin, and fix the Standard of Weights and Measures;

"To provide for the Punishment of counterfeiting the Securities and current Coin of the United States;

"To establish Post Offices and post Roads;

"To promote the Progress of Science and the useful Arts, by securing for limited Times to Authors and Inventors the exclusive Right to their respective Writings and Discoveries; . . .

"To declare War, grant Letters of Marque and Reprisal, and make Rules concerning Captures on Land and Water;

"To raise and support Armies; . . .

"To provide and maintain a Navy," and in order that authority may be adequate to its objective, the power

"To make all Laws which shall be necessary and proper for carrying into Execution the foregoing Powers."

Here in their fullness are the powers of the eighteenth-century state. If "general Welfare" does not appear as a clause apart, it is resolved into the powers which the people of the times regarded as essential to its attainment. Moreover, it appears at the head of the list in association with such objects of primary concern as the collection of revenue, the payment of debts, and the provision for the common "Defence." All of them relate to a competitive nationalism whose principal instruments are war and commerce. All are concerned in their several ways with the promotion of the activities which the people of the times called commerce. Even in its most restricted sense the power of Congress over Commerce is a matter of no single clause; in every item set down above is an aspect of its multiple regulation.

And, as only solemn intent can explain, the powers extend to every aspect of commerce which was current.

5. Orbits for the States

A "free communication" among the delegates revealed the demand for a strong government. It was required as "a shield against foreign hostility and a firm resort against domestic commotion." [79] National power was to be had only by curbing the authority of states which might be "intoxicated with the idea" of their new won "sovereignty." [80] The Convention opens on the lofty theme of great national purpose; the counter theme of the rights of the states, at first a small voice, swells with the political demands of the small states and as their place in the structure of the government is fixed, dies away again. It is never evoked by a discussion of the powers of Congress. The deliberations close on the national note on which they opened.

The scanty records abound in suggestions of the intent of the Fathers. Mr. Wilson, whose turn of mind was democratic, hoped "a foederal Government may be established that will insure freedom and yet be vigorous." Mr. Pinckney, of the Southern planters, was certain that unless "the influence of the States" is lost, "we never shall have anything like a national institution." [81] Mr. Gouverneur Morris insisted that "the Feebleness of the general Government" will be "in proportion to the

Vigor and Strength of State Governments." Mr. Madison, who would have the states reduced to counties or turned into administrative districts, saw "the prerogative of the General Government" as "the great pervading principle that must controul the centrifugal tendency of the States; which, without it, will continually fly out of their proper orbits and destroy the order and harmony of the political system." [82] And Mr. Randolph at least suggested in the secrecy of the executive session that "the states as states must be cut up," for "we ought to be one Nation." [83]

Such extreme views did not prevail. The new commonwealths were too vigorous to give way completely before national authority; as established institutions they could be caught up within the fabric of the newer government. Mr. Wilson conceded that the States "were absolutely necessary for certain purposes" which the national government "could not reach." [84] Mr. Pinckney admitted that the general Government "cannot effectively exist without reserving to the States . . . their local rights." [85] And Randolph, with utopian hopes tempered to reality, insisted that he "only meant to give to the National Government power to defend and protect itself—to take, therefore, from the respective Legislatures of States no more sovereignty than is competent to this end." [86] The national authority had to stretch across several hundred miles of territory; the poor communication limited the effective reach of its arm; the states were necessary to suit administration to local conditions.

The government which emerged was of its own kind. It was, with the Confederation as a model, not Federal. The "extent of its authority" was not to be fixed by "requisitions upon the Confederated States" nor to rest "on the sanctions of State Legislatures." Instead it "was to operate within the extent of its powers directly and coercively on individuals, and to receive the higher sanction of the people of the States." [87] But it was, with the Kingdom of Great Britain as a standard, something less than national. In fact it partook of the quality of both.[88] For the States had insinuated themselves into the political structure, and the powers entrusted to the general government were national in their scope. Such was "the proper correspondence of sentiments" which emerged from protracted conferences among the delegates.

The limitation of the state to its proper orbit appears in the discussion of the provision prohibiting any state to "lay duties on imports or exports." Mr. Mason, as a mercantilist and a Virginian, was unwilling to have his state give up its power to shape its own commercial destiny. He insisted that "particular states might wish to encourage by import duties certain manufactures, for which they enjoyed natural advantages." [89] Mr. Madison, as a mercantilist of national persuasions, could not agree with Mr. Mason; for "the encouragement of manufacture" by separate state action required duties, not only on imports from abroad, but also upon articles from other states of the Union; and the result would be the perpetuation of "all the mischiefs experienced from the want of a general government over commerce." Mr. Morris heartily approved, since some such provision was necessary "to prevent the Atlantic States from endeavoring to tax the Western States."

But Mr. Clymer of Pennsylvania was afraid that "the encouragement of the Western Country was suicide on the old States" and was certain that if states with different interests "cannot be left to regulate their own manufactures without encountering the interests of other States, it is a proof that they are not fit to compose one nation." And Mr. King added that stripping them of power over imports and exports "would too much interfere with a policy of States respecting their manufactures." With Massachusetts and Maryland alone dissenting, the delegates proceeded to adopt the provision. As a body they were in accord with Madison, who was "more and more convinced that the regulation of Commerce was in its nature indivisible and ought to be wholly under one authority." [90] Thus the delegates forbade the states the use of import duties "to regulate" commerce, "to encourage" manufacture, to shape an economy.

Nor did the matter stop here. The states must not be permitted to impose rules or to levy tolls upon mer-

chandise passing across its borders under the pretext of
inspection laws. A motion by Mr. Sherman, a debate on
the floor, and a formulation by the Committee of Stile
produced the clause, "No state shall, without the consent of Congress, lay imposts or duties on imports or
exports, nor with such consent but to the use of the
Treasury of the United States." Mr. Mason,[91] returning
to the defense of a state mercantilism, insisted that this
provision would "prevent the incidental duties necessary
for the inspection and safekeeping of . . . produce."
Mr. Madison felt that export duties for inspection purposes would be "harmless." It seemed to him that "perhaps the best guard against an abuse of the power of
the States on this subject, was the right in the General
Government to regulate trade between State and State."
But Mr. Dayton of New Jersey and Mr. Langdon of
New Hampshire had seen "the oppression" of their
states by neighboring commonwealths; and Mr. Gorham
wanted to know how "redress was to be obtained in
case duties should be laid beyond the purpose expressed."
A flurry of debate, a concession by Mason,[92] a report
out of Committee and it was finally agreed that "No
State shall, without the Consent of the Congress, lay
any Imposts or Duties on Imports or Exports, except
what may be absolutely necessary for executing its inspection Laws; and the net Produce of all Duties and
Imposts, laid by any State on Imports or Exports, shall
be for the Use of the Treasury of the United States;

and all such Laws shall be subject to the Revision and Controul of the Congress." From the temptation to use duties as a means of raising revenue or regulating commerce the states were utterly delivered.[93]

So, too, were they enjoined in other respects from an intermeddling at the expense of the performance of national offices. In the emerging Constitution it was set down that "No State shall

Enter into any Treaty, Alliance, or Confederation; grant letters of Marque and Reprisal;
coin Money;
make any Thing but gold and silver a Tender in Payment of Debts;
pass any Bill of Attainder, ex post facto Law, or Law impairing the obligation of Contracts, or grant any Title of Nobility."

The appearance on the list of "Bill of Attainder" and "Title of Nobility" throws into sharp relief the concern of the other items with matters commercial. In short, a policy for the direction of a national economy was put beyond the reach of the separate commonwealths.

In the debates the presumption is that trade purely local in character was to be left to the states; but nowhere is such a stipulation set down in writing. Aside from the word "among"—which means of concern "to more than one State," [94]—the supreme law of the land contains nothing to limit the national jurisdiction. Nor

are the debates much richer in evidence of such an intent. The terms "inter-state" and "intra-state" were then
unknown; the thought of the age recognized the organic
character of commercial activity; and the Fathers were
not in the habit of severing with mechanical lines aspects
of a living whole. The available testimony yields no evidence of a demand for a separation of dominions between state and nation.[95] On the contrary, in respect to
powers over commerce, the states are in the position of
subordinate authorities. As Mr. Wilson put it, "Whatever object of government extends in its operation or
effect beyond the bounds of a particular State should be
considered as belonging to the Government of the
United States." [96] The larger principles carved into specific powers pointed the way. The Congress might legislate "in the general interests," where the several states
were "incompetent," or where separate action was a
threat to the harmony of the Union. Such acts were, as
is usual with nations, to take precedence over local ordinances. So a later danger was anticipated and guarded
against in a single sentence of classic simplicity. "This
Constitution, and the Laws of the United States which
shall be made in Pursuance thereof . . . shall be the
supreme Law of the Land." A simple rule of priority
was proof against dual sovereignty and jurisdictional
conflict.

There remained the question of an effective instrument. On numerous occasions Mr. Madison had insisted

that "a negative" by Congress "on the State laws alone
could meet all the shapes" which the intrusive acts of
the separate commonwealths "could assume." [97] He had
his formidable band of followers; but, although agreeing
to his principle, the Convention could not accept his
instrument. The Congress was not to be in continuous
session; the attention it could give to the matter was
limited; the acts of state legislatures flowed in a continuous stream. The device suggested by Madison was
slow, clumsy, and ill-adapted to its purpose. It was, in
the finished Constitution, replaced by a flexible instrument neatly suited to its purpose. The matter of accommodation was to be left to the judiciary. The discretion
as to what was national or local in character was left
to Congress; and, in matters of conflict, "the Judges in
every State shall be bound" to give validity to "the Laws
of the United States which shall be made in Pursuance"
of the Constitution, "anything in the Constitution or
Laws of any State to the Contrary notwithstanding."
The unified domain in authority, the priority of national
legislation, and the obligation imposed upon the judiciary are all clear—according to the Constitution.[98]

Always—everywhere—the ideas of the political economy popular to the times were in evidence. Whatever
the concern of the debates—the distrust of aliens, the
dominion of commerce, the regulatory character of
taxes, the control of bankruptcies, the merits of sumptuary legislation—the spirit of the nationalism of trade

prevailed. In all the debates there is little cleavage along
the line of idea, theory, or philosophy. One group, with
staple crops to give direction to argument, would repair
the breach in the old imperial economy caused by the
Revolution. Another, with a prospective interest in the
encouragement of manufactures, would build an autono-
mous American economy. The difference was in pattern; the systems were like expressions of the prevailing
common sense of mercantilism.

· VI ·

A High-Toned Government

1. *The Power over Powers*

THE DEMAND for a general control over commerce goes back to the days of the Revolution. As early as 1778, General George Washington had written that "unless the States will" vest the Congress "with absolute power in all matters relating to the great purpose of war and of general concern" we "are attempting an impossibility." [1] In 1783, with the country at peace, he wrote, "To suppose that the great concerns of this country can be directed by thirteen heads, or one head without competent powers, is a solecism." [2] In 1787 a letter formulated by the Committee of Detail and bearing his name was dispatched, transmitting to the Congress "that Constitution which has appeared to us the most advisable." In its words, "The friends of our country have long seen and desired, that the power of making war, peace and treaties, that of levying money and regulating commerce . . . should be fully and effectively vested in the general government of the Union." [3] Such a grant of powers, for all its novelty and magnitude, provoked surprisingly little opposition in the Convention. The great debate came upon questions as to who was to command so powerful an instrument of government.

In a letter to his son in England written a year after the Convention, Pierce Butler wondered—without the slightest taint of treason—if the New England States had really bettered themselves through the separation from Great Britain. Their position in the fishing trade off the Banks had not been improved; they had been deprived of participation in the Empire carrying trade; they had lost "many other benefits that they had in common with the British under your Navigation Laws and wise Commercial System." All that "our Brethren of the Eastern States" had gained "by a long and bloody conflict," has been "the honor of calling themselves independent States." [4] The South, on the contrary, had more substantial advantages; freights had become cheaper to a great increase in the profits on tobacco, rice, and indigo. Here was a subject for sectional conflict.

In a letter to Thomas Jefferson, written in the same year, Madison states, "Wherever the real power in a Government lies, there is the danger of oppression. In our Governments the real power lies in the majority of the Community, and the invasion of private rights is *chiefly* to be apprehended . . . from acts in which the Government is the mere instrument of the major number of the constituents." [5] Here is the fear of the people and a problem for the Convention.

The Convention was hardly at work before the sectional issue broke. In so far as Randolph's plan proposed a reorganization of the American economy on a national plan, it met no opposition. But when, as a spokesman for Virginia, he proposed that this authority be exercised by a Congress, in which the several states had representation in proportion to their numbers, he touched off a sudden conflict.

The larger and the smaller states at once divided on the principle of proportional representation. It was clear to Delaware, Maryland, Connecticut, New Jersey, and New York that such a device would put their interests at a tremendous disadvantage. It would insure to "the big three" of Massachusetts, Pennsylvania, and Virginia the dominant influence in the councils of the government. In the Confederation each state had stood as an equal among equals; under "the new roof" the small states would become satellites revolving about the greater suns.

But a protest against fitting representation to numbers was not an opposition to a national control of the economy. All agreed that it was high time for American trade to be prudently regulated, for resources to be efficiently managed, and for the country's credit to be re-established. It was evident "the three great objects of government, *agriculture, commerce and revenue,* can only be secured by a general government." [6] But a new model of government was not necessary; instead the little-state men insisted that vesting in the existing Congress powers to regulate commerce and to tax would in itself infuse the Union with "vigor and strength." As Mr. Paterson, the spear-head of the small-state drive, saw it, "regulation of commerce, Collec. of revenue, Negative on the state legislatures" [7] would draw after it "such a Weight and Power as will answer the Purpose." [8] And in the exercise of the authority the vote of New Jersey would still be equal to that of Virginia.

Mr. Randolph was quick to meet the attack. He asked whether the control of commerce—a power important in its very nature—could safely be entrusted to a body so unworthy and impotent as the existing Congress. "Every one is impressed," he declared, "with the idea of the general regulation of trade and commerce"; but "can congress do this? when from the nature of their institution they are so subject to cabal and intrigue?" [9] Lansing of New York, invoking scruples to support his firmness, was convinced that only a strengthening of the present Union [10] would meet with "public concurrence." Mr. Mason of Virginia was of a contrary mind. He was certain that any plan which proposed to augment the powers of the existing Congress "never could be expected to succeed." He was careful to explain that he did not mean "to throw any reflections on Congress, . . . much less on any particular members of it," but it was inconceivable that the people of America, "so jealous of their liberties, will give up their all, will surrender both the sword and the purse, to the same body, and that, too, not immediately chosen by themselves. They never will. They never ought." It was pure moonshine to expect that the great electorate—which must eventually pass upon the work of the Convention—would "trust such a body with the regulation of their trade, with the regulation of their taxes; with all the other great powers which are in contemplation." [11] And, as the battle over representation reached its climax, Mr. Wilson spoke to the same effect. "We have unanimously agreed to establish a general government" and it had without dissent been resolved "that the powers of peace, war, treaties, coinage, and regulating of commerce, ought to reside in that government." [12]

It had been argued for the smaller commonwealths that, if they gave up their equality, they would lose their liberty. In the heat of the debate Mr. Hamilton bluntly declared, "The truth is, it is a contest for power, not for liberty." [13] Mr. Pinckney was brutally frank and to the point, "The whole comes to this, as he conceived. Give N. Jersey an equal vote, and she will dismiss her scruples, and concur in the Natl. system." [14] The bitterness of the contest sprang from the greatness of the power at issue. The stake for which the tiers of states battled was an authority to foster or to hinder the economic activities of interest and of section. It was only by

participation in the exercise of that power that, as an
inferior part of a greater whole, a state could safeguard
the particular sources of its opulence. As Mr. Bedford,
delegate from Delaware, put it, "Delaware would [under
proportional representation] have about one-ninetieth
for its share in the General Councils, whilst Pennsylvania and Virginia would possess one-third of the
whole." He asked, "Is there no difference of interests,
no rivalship of commerce, of manufactures? Will not
these large States crush the small ones whenever they
stand in the way of their ambitious or interested
views?" [15]

Mr. Madison could not discover such a threat. In
respect to the big states he vainly insisted that "their
situation is remote, their trade different. The staple of
Massachusetts is fish, and the carrying trade—of Pennsylvania, wheat and flour—of Virginia, tobacco. Can States
thus situated in trade ever form such a combination?" [16]
Col. Hamilton pointed out that division in commercial
matters did not break along the line of large as against
small states; that "the only considerable distinction of
interests lay between the carrying and non-carrying
States," and in this respect the interests of the largest
states were divided rather than united. [17] And Mr. Williamson of North Carolina, looking into the future, saw
that there was no finality as to what states were to be
large or small. He envisioned "new States from the
Westward," small, poor, [18] and "unable to pay in propor-

tion to their numbers," which in the future would be tempted "to combine for the purpose of laying burdens on commerce and consumption which would fall with greatest weight on the old States." [19] Would the Convention write into their system the two-edged sword of equal state representation which in time to come might be used with such disastrous effect on the present states irrespective of size?

The delegates from the small states most certainly would; such arguments about the future were not to still their present fears. They were suspicious of such protestations of disinterestedness by the great; they were not soothed by the insistence that there can be no united front among the strong. Mr. Ellsworth did not think the "danger of combinations" among the big states "imaginary." He was willing to admit that "no particular abuses could be foreseen by him"; but, as a man of abstract imagination, "he could easily conceive cases in which they might result from such combinations." And, as a representative of Connecticut, the "possibility" was "sufficient to alarm him." [20]

Tempers were growing short. Ellsworth went on to call attention to the existing "federal compact . . . entered into with so much solemnity," and argued that some regard should "be paid to the plighted faith under which each State small as well as great, held an equal right of suffrage in the General Councils." Mr. Madison's retort descended to personalities. Then for a brief

instant the assembled Convention witnessed the spec-
tacle of the Virginian and the Connecticut delegates on
their feet shouting at each other. The Virginian charged
that reference to the plighted faith of the Confederation
came with poor taste from Connecticut, a state notorious
in its violations of Congressional requisitions. Ellsworth
retorted that Connecticut had put more men in the field
during the Revolution than had Virginia.

It was the venerable Franklin who rose to act as medi-
ator. A proposal of compromise had been put forward
by Mr. Sherman of Connecticut.[21] Franklin now saw a
chance to persuade the delegates to accept it. "When a
broad table is to be made, and the edges of planks do not
fit the artist takes a little from both and makes a good
joint." Let us have one House elected proportionally,
but in order to give the small states the security they
demand, let us have equal suffrage in the other. Both
parties "must part with some of their demands" that we
may join in some accommodating proposition. But Mr.
King of Massachusetts would not surrender. The ob-
stinacy of the small states ready to sacrifice everything
"to the phantom of state sovereignty" was beyond belief.
He could not accept a government founded on the
"vicious principle" of equal suffrage. And to his support
came Mr. Madison.

Then Mr. Bedford of Delaware—a man "warm and
impetuous in his nature"—sprang to his feet. In language
whose most distinctive quality was not restraint, he flung

out the challenge, "*I do not, gentlemen, trust you.* If you possess the power the abuse of it could not be checked. . . . You gravely allege that there is no danger of combination . . . that instead" the large States "would be rivals and counteract the views of one another. This, I repeat, is language calculated only to amuse us. Yes, sir, the larger States will be rivals, but not against each other—they will be rivals against the *rest of the States.*" As delegates, we have a specific mandate from the people who have "said, 'We find the confederation defective—go, and give additional powers to the confederation—give to it the imposts, regulation of trade, power to collect the taxes, and the means to discharge our foreign and domestic debts.' Can we not then, as their delegates, agree upon these points?" Then he threatened, "Sooner than be ruined, there are foreign powers who will take us by the hand." [22]

With the Convention deadlocked it was a choice between compromise or no constitution. Over July 4th a committee worked over the proposal and recommended the compromise as the only solution. The delegates from the large states were not reconciled; and, although they must have realized that they were beaten, for two weeks they kept up a desperate rear-guard action. Randolph offered to specify certain subjects on which all states would have an equal vote,[23] and there was some talk of a representation based on wealth; but when, on August 16th, the final vote came the small states had won their point. Proportional representation was set down for the House and in the Senate the several states were given— even against a later amendment—equal votes. A few irreconcilables among the large-state bloc, led by Randolph, refused to accept the decision as final. The majority, however, as Madison reports, agreed "to yield to the smaller States and to concur in such an Act however imperfect & exceptionable" [24] as might be worked out by the now united Convention.

In the discussion unity and conflict had distinctive roles. Interest, group, and state had a tremendous stake in a high-toned government; no party or faction could willingly surrender such a command to neighbor or competitor. No principle of abstract political thought divided the delegates into two schools; they had no differences as to the functions and powers of the new government. Paterson, Sherman and the little-state men believed as firmly as did Hamilton and the Virginians that the power to shape the country's economy is an attribute of national sovereignty. The debates reflect the accepted notions of the best of eighteenth-century political economy. The protest of the small states was against assignment to a minor role in a drama of power.

A design of point and counterpoint runs through the proceedings up to the Great Compromise. The theme of the necessity of national control has as accompaniment the recurring fears of the small states. It was the unanimity about powers that gave play to the conflict over their possession.

The question of the rights of "the minority" prompted less conflict. The excesses of popular government had led to a reaction; the delegates were in general opposed to leveling laws; and care was to be taken that the general government should be "capable of protecting the rights of property against the spirit of democracy." [25] To Mr. Morris "property was the main object of Society" and "could only be secured by the restraints of regular Government"; he scorned the "inaccurate" views of those that held "life and liberty" to be of more value. These were the "sentiments precisely" of Mr. Rutledge.[26] Mr. King of Massachusetts, too, was in accord; "property was the primary object of society" and Mr. Butler in agreement apostrophized it as "the great object of Government; the great cause of war; and the great means of carrying it on." [27] The shadow of Shays' rebellion and the threat of civic strife fall across the pages; the Property of the Minority must be safeguarded against the Voice of the Majority.

If the objective had been an exemption of the rights of property from legislative control,[28] it could have been easily effected. A prohibition against "leveling" statutes by the national government or a limitation upon the police of the several states would have served the occasion. This would have been the way of champions of a policy of *laissez-faire* in the late Nineteenth Century.

But such a path was not open to their minds; the prevailing belief in the duty of the State to turn competitive national advantage to account blocked so negative a course. Mr. Wilson expressed the general sentiment that "there are only two kinds of bad governments—the one which does *too much* and [is] therefore oppressive, and the other which does *too little* and [is] therefore weak." There was general agreement that the Congress of the Confederation "partakes of the latter." [29] To the delegates it was imperative to set up a government that could take positive action for the encouragement of commerce and the conservation of property. The great obstacle was that the people could not be trusted with the necessary powers. They were incapable of a sustained and forward-looking policy, and in respect to property they lacked proper regard for its sanctity.

Thus the necessity for national power and the distrust of the people are the terms of the problem with which the delegates were confronted. They evolved a practical solution. They would not limit, by definition and qualification, a broad Congressional power over commerce and taxation. Accordingly they had to devise ways of keeping so great an authority out of the reach of the masses. Their ingenuity rose to the occasion. The Congress which was to govern was very carefully constituted. A balance was established between the aristocratic Senate and the democratic House. The threat of rule by a popular majority was broken by a purposive scheme of election. The House was to be elected by persons qualified to vote for members of the more numerous branch of the state legislatures; the Senators were to be elected by the legislatures of the several States. The President was to be selected by electors chosen solely for the purpose. The short terms of two years went to the House; the longer ones of six years to the Senate. There could be no overturn of the whole body of legislators at a single election. The whole scheme was designed to refract different interests and classes so that minorities—especially if made up of men of substance and standing—were to be free from the tyranny of majorities.[30]

In the checks and balances of its studied mechanism the electoral system seemed to promise power without danger. The delegates were aware that authority could not be insulated against the persons who must command it. To them the best insurance against its abuse was to entrust it to the best people, that is, to men of property. As Mr. Mercer declared, "it is a great mistake to suppose that the paper we are to propose will govern the U. States. It is the men whom it will bring into the Government and interest in maintaining it that is to govern them. The paper will only mark out the mode and the form. Men are the substance and must do the business." [31] It was all put neatly enough in the heat of the campaign for the ratification of the Constitution, "Public views were to be refined and enlarged by passing them through the medium of a chosen body of citizens." [32] A painstaking attention to detail had woven a scheme for the protection of the rights of property into the very structure of the government. A "fence" had been erected against the abuse of broad powers—and without benefit of rigid definition and paralyzing prohibition.

It was a republic, not a democracy, which the Founders were to establish. In the language of their day a democracy was a state after the pattern in use in classic Athens and early Rome, a polity in which the people legislate and govern in their own persons. Its application to continental America was as impossible as it was unwise. To them a republic was a government entrusted to a small number of citizens elected by the rest. It gave opportunity to the people to act through representatives. It was to be the rule of those who were fit to rule— landlords, merchants, planters, lawyers, and men of substance and standing. Under the Constitution the United States was to be a government of men as well as of laws.

2. *The Gauntlet of Scrutiny*

An entry in the diary of the First Citizen of the United States records the end—and the beginning—of an event. "Met in convention when the Constitution received the unanimous assent of 11 States and Colo. Hamilton's. . . . The business being thus closed, the Members . . . dined together and took a cordial leave of each other—after which I returned to my lodgings . . . and retired to meditate on the momentous wk. which had been executed." [33]

In truth, however, the business was not closed nor the work executed. The Constitution, drawn up in executive session, had to run the gauntlet of a skeptical public scrutiny. It had to command the approval of conventions in at least nine of the states before its provisions could become the supreme law of the land.

To the great mass of people, entrenched behind the security of the domestic economy, it might present only a question of academic interest or a problem for the future. Yet where it escaped indifference it ran into hostility. In a raw untamed country a sturdy self-reliance is the price of survival; the rights of man are no bundle of abstractions; and the voice of authority is not a categorical imperative. The proposal of a high-toned government was certain to be met with suspicion and hostility; and the ordinary American, outside the money economy, was particularly fearful of power in fields in which his ancestors had experienced oppression. Nor was this attitude confined to the back-country; settled communities were not far removed in time, and still less in thought, from the frontier.

To those immediately concerned it was different. To city-dwellers and the moneyed interest it brought the call to a decision upon a national destiny. A conservative group was sure the old government, buttressed with an up-to-date prop or two, was quite adequate. A band of perfectionists, admitting that "the people of this country cannot change their constitution for the worse," were intent "to endeavor deliberately to change it for the better." [34] Few were quite satisfied; yet practical men generally were disposed, in spite of its many shortcomings, to accept the new instrument as a significant step in the right direction. In speech and pamphlet the hope of the national adventure, the advantages of a high-toned government, and the dangers lurking in harmless-looking propositions were everywhere debated.

In a voluminous literature, which can hardly be adequately sampled, the authority of the new government to shape the economy of the country received general attention. The newspapers divided sharply; neither advocate of the new nationalism nor champion of the established Confederation had doubts in the chosen faith. In behalf of the Constitution an appeal was directed to the interests which made up the nation. The mercantile interest has suffered enough to induce them to "espouse a federal reform"; if the proposals are accepted, "commerce may then become a national object." The mechanical interest "can have no aversion to it, when they are informed that an efficient government will protect and encourage commerce, which is the very soul of mechanism"; besides it is not to their advantage "to quarrel with their bread and butter." Nor can "the honest farmer have any objection"; the "prosperity of commerce gives vent to his produce" and "raises the value of his lands"; he will be able to pay his taxes and, "if economy shakes hands with industry, increase his farm and live independent of troublesome creditors." [35] Throughout the country "every enterprise, public as well as private," seemed "suspended until we know what kind of Government we are to receive." [36] In anxiety all who trafficked in commerce were forced to abide the event.

A roster of the ratifying conventions of the several states offers numerous variations upon the theme of ratification. In Massachusetts issues were brought into the open, provisions were probed for hidden promise and threat, and federalist and republican battled sturdily to command the result. Mr. Bowdoin staged a parade of the "notorious sufferings" of the states "for the want of a general regulation of trade." The continent "is being exhausted of its wealth; instead of regulating trade upon principle; instead of improving the natural advantages of our country, and opening new sources of wealth, our lands have sunk in their value, our trade has languished, our credit has been daily reducing, and our resources are almost annihilated." "The well-being of trade depends on a proper regulation of it; on the success of trade depends wealth; on wealth, the value of lands . . . the happiness of a country . . . Trade, for the want of its being confined to proper objects, has served rather to ruin than to enrich those that have carried it on." [37] And, discarding statement for rhetorical question, he asked, "Will the people long continue their allegiance to systems . . . which entail on them so many calamities?"

In time a number of anti-federalists lost patience with the reiterated linking of union and prosperity. Mr. Widgery, of New Gloucester, bitterly complained that "it had been repeated over and over again that the adoption of the Constitution will please all ranks; that the present inefficiency of the Confederation is obvious; and that blessed things will surely be the result of the Constitution." He added, "All we hear is, that the merchant and farmer will flourish, and that mechanics and tradesmen are to make their fortunes directly, if the Constitution goes down." [38]

Mr. Singletary felt called upon to deliver even keener words of protest. "These lawyers and men of learning, and moneyed men, that talk so finely, and gloss over matters so smoothly to make us poor illiterate people swallow down the pill, expect to get into Congress themselves; they expect to be the managers of this Constitution and get all the power and all the money into their own hands, and then they will swallow up all us little folks, like the great *Leviathan*, Mr. President; yes, just as the whale swallowed up *Jonah*." [39]

In South Carolina the same vista of ratification and prosperity was opened for the benefit of the skeptical. Many Southerners regarded the instrument as a surrender of the agrarian interests of the South to the commercial

North. In answer Pinckney persuasively stressed the interdependence of merchant and planter. He did not believe with Franklin that commerce "is generally cheating." On the contrary "some kinds of commerce" were "not only fair and valuable, but such as ought to be encouraged by government." He did feel, however, that "Poor Richard" was correct "in his general principle—that all great objects of government should be subservient to the increase of agriculture and the support of the landed interest, and that commerce should only be so far attended to, as it may serve to improve and strengthen them." [40] The sovereignty to be erected by the Constitution would in Mr. Pinckney's judgment be ever mindful of this general principle.

In North Carolina the debates were marked by the same clash of interests. The burden of the argument for ratification was the inestimable benefits to the State from an invigorated trade. According to Mr. Davie the "general object of the Union" was "1st, to protect us against foreign invasion; 2d, to defend us against internal commotions and insurrections; 3d, to promote the commerce, agriculture, and manufactures of America . . . Commerce, sir, is the nurse of both. The merchant furnishes the planter with such articles as he cannot manufacture himself, and finds him a market for his produce. Agriculture cannot flourish if commerce languishes; they are mutually dependent on each other. Our commerce" is "without regulation at home" and many of the States are "ruined by partial and iniquitous laws which basely" warrant and legalize "the payment of just debts by paper." The new government "should be empowered to compel foreign nations into commercial regulations that" are "either founded upon the principles of justice or reciprocal advantages." And, linking the powers over war and trade, "is not our commerce equally unprotected abroad by arms and negotiations?" [41]

As a consolation to advocates of local government, concessions were made. Southern delegates were assured that there was a complete "security" in their possession of slaves; that the Congress "has no powers but what are expressly granted by the Constitution." [42] There was "not one instance" of a power given to "the general government" whereby the internal policy or administration of the States is affected. [43] But Mr. Patrick Henry in Virginia begged the delegates to put first things first. "You are not to enquire how your trade may be increased nor how you are to become a great and powerful people, but how your liberties can be secured; for liberty ought to be the direct end of your government." [44] And to Mr. Lenoir in North Carolina, shuddering at the departure of freedom from the land, it seemed "that instead of securing the sovereignty of the States, it [was] calculated to melt them down in one solid empire." [45] It was this feeling that made the fear of the executive so strong and that finally extorted a Bill of Rights. These discussions were all but a session of the Convention, for out of them emerged the first Ten Amendments. Support and attack are alike in endowing the general government with the attributes of national sovereignty; they differ only in a preference as between a recitation of blessings and a parade of horribles.

An epitome of the case for the Constitution appears in the series of papers called the *Federalist*. Here popular support is distilled into a convincing appeal; opposition is routed beneath a barrage of reasons; and a persuasive argument is set in the key of lofty national purpose. The interests of groups and of parties are inseparable from the destiny of the Nation. It is a "disgrace to human nature," yet a world of hostile nations will close in with commerce and war upon the separate and divided states. In the fisheries the United States are rivals of Great Britain and France; it will be "more their policy to restrain than to promote the carrying trade"; we are "cutting into the China and India trade" which they had "in a manner monopolized." Spain had already closed to the States the Mississippi, and Great Britain the St. Lawrence. Foreign powers will resist with every device of statecraft the national advantages which lie in "the cheapness and excellence of our productions" and "the enterprise and address of our merchants and navigators." Against a competitive nationalism a strength which can nourish and protect the interests which make up the state lies in union alone.[46]

It is all, in march of argument, in pointed instance, in

promise and threat, a practical gospel of nationalism. It aimed to translate general propositions into concretions which every man could understand and to bring home to particular interests the specific advantages which the Constitution held out to them. Its reiterated beat upon the necessity for union, the power of Congress over commerce, the hazard to independence, is always topical, always of the occasion, always pointed to the interest. In the present instance "the profits of trade are snatched from us; our commerce languishes; and poverty threatens to over-spread a country which might outrival the world in riches." [47] It follows that the one requisite to strength and opulence is "a vigorous national government." Under it "the natural strength and resources of the country, directed to a common interest, would baffle all the combinations of European jealousy to restrain our growth." Under it "an active commerce, an extensive navigation, and a flourishing marine would then be the offspring of moral and physical necessity." Thus equipped "we might defy the little arts of the little politicians to control or vary the irresistible and unchangeable course of nature." [48] If foreign powers see "our national government is efficient and well-administered, our trade prudently regulated, our militia properly organized and disciplined, our credit reestablished," they will be "more disposed to cultivate our friendship than provoke our resentment." Union will put us "in such a situation as, instead of inviting war, will tend to replace and discourage it."

A touch of the absolute of theory seasons the concrete march of the argument. The new instrument of government has "silenced the rivalries that once subsisted" between "agriculture and commerce." It "has proved, to the satisfaction of their friends, that their interests are intimately blended and interwoven." [49] We may, "by prohibitory regulations" which extend throughout the States, "oblige foreign countries to bid against each other for the privilege of our markets." [50] The "regulations of the mere domestic police of a State appears . . . to hold out slender allurements to ambition. Commerce, finance, negotiation, and war seem to comprehend all the objects which have charms for minds governed by that passion; and all the powers necessary to those objects ought, in the first instance, to be lodged in the national depositary." [51] Nationalism is the only path that leads away from civil war, loss of independence, and foreign dismemberment.

3. *From Polemic to Practice*

A vast body of circumstantial evidence conspires to endow the words of the Constitution with the gloss of contemporary meaning. It is impossible here to explore the whole domain of pamphlet and polemic, of document and broadside. Even a sparse sampling would overcrowd the pages to which such indirect evidence must be confined. A few representative items must do duty for a vast body of dialectical literature and official utterance.

It may be that "not a scrap of evidence" has survived to link the name of Peletiah Webster with the immortal document. But his "Dissertation on the Political Union . . . of the Thirteen United States" appeared more than four years before the Convention; the ways of his mind are those of influential delegates; and suggestions of his are newly born in the debates. At the very least his pamphlet is a concurrent expression of the political thought of the age addressed to a national crisis. His "first and great principle" is "that the Constitution must vest powers in every department sufficient to secure and make effectual the ends of it." In language prophetic of the event he states that "the supreme authority must have the power of making war and peace—of appointing armies and navies—of appointing officers both civil and military—of making contracts—of emitting, coining and borrowing money—of regulating trade—of making treaties with foreign powers—of establishing post-offices —and in short of doing everything which the well-being of the commonwealth may require, and which is not compatible to any particular State." He adds that "the powers of Congress . . . shall . . . be restricted to such matters only of general necessity and utility . . . as cannot come within the jurisdiction of any particular State, or to which the authority of any particular State is not competent." [52]

But no such challenge can be lodged against the testimony of Tench Coxe. In a document whose renown has hardly reflected its quality, he presents an overture to the coming debates. He was an economist of note, the friend and adviser of public men, and a delegate to the Annapolis Convention. He was later to win a vicarious immortality as a literary aide in the preparation of Hamilton's *Report on Manufactures*.[53] A paper of his, dubbed with the title, "An Inquiry into the Principles on which a Commercial System for the United States of America should be Founded; to which are added some Observations connected with the Subject," was read to a small group gathered at the home of Dr. Benjamin Franklin on May 11, 1787. Later, while the Convention was sitting, it was issued as a pamphlet and circulated among the delegates.[54]

The note of the essay is a call to decision. He points the paradox of a nation endowed with such superlative natural advantages that it could surpass the world in prosperity reduced to a most "painful situation." All the requisites of national wealth—a fertile soil, a climate admitting of steady labor, abundant land, "cheap enough to tempt the European from his home and the manufacturer from his trade"—are to be found here. Agriculture under the circumstances is the leading interest—employing "at least nine parts in ten of the inhabitants" and not only "furnishes a spring to our commerce, and the parent of our manufactures" but also "promotes the health and morality" of the citizenry "by keeping our people from the luxuries and vices of the towns."

But all these active benefits and future blessings hang in the balance. This is the "crisis" when "exertion or neglect must produce consequences of the utmost moment." Money is "absorbed by a wanton consumption of imported luxuries"; a fluctuating paper currency is being substituted for specie, foreign commerce is "extremely circumscribed." Both the cause and the cure of the economic evil, Coxe felt, lay in the political sphere. Our government is "not only ineffective but disjointed." It is not a matter of alternatives; patriotism and sound policy "requires" a national commercial system for the United States.

The "commerce of America, including our exports, imports, shipping, manufactures, and fisheries may be properly considered as forming one interest." From it is to be expected no threat to men on the land, no fear of dominance in the councils of the nation. Even in New England, the most "commercial quarter of the Union," it accounts for less than one-eighth of the population.[55] In the country at large the disproportion is much larger; for "several of the states have little commerce and no manufactures—others have no commerce and scarcely manufacture anything." Agriculture is and should be our leading interest. Timber, iron, cordage are necessary to fishing, to trading, to ship-building. The raw materials which are "the product of our lands" are "the subsistence" of our "manufacturers." In all the countries of Europe "judicious writers have considered commerce as the handmaid of agriculture"; in America the relationship is "unquestionable."

But though there can be no question as to "the great superiority" of landed interest over all the others combined, we must give "every encouragement to commerce and its connexions—the fisheries and manufactures." The true interests of the land demand "a system of commercial regulations." Carefully established it will do nothing to "interrupt the happy progress" of our agricultural affairs; all the policies we embark on to enrich our country must be "consistent with a due regard to agriculture" and in no way "prejudicial to this great mass of property and to this great body of the people."

In this spirit of conciliation he proceeds to positive recommendations. The coastwise trade should be secured to "the domestic navigation of our own people." A duty, or even a "prohibition, of foreign articles, such as our own fisheries supply, will be safe and expedient"—and a protective blow at Nova Scotia.[56] He suggests that the Convention copy the article from the British Acts of Trade and Navigation which confines the importation of foreign goods to the bottoms of the countries producing them. But he warns that the restrictions and prohibitions which affect particular nations must be shaped with great prudence.

It is, however, to manufacture that he points his argument. It is a pigmy compared with the giant agriculture; the opulence of America lies in the land. Yet already "there is a valuable body of manufactures here, and many more will emigrate from Europe." In addition a supply of labor is available in "citizens so poor as not to be able to effect a little settlement on our waste lands." The whole matter invites "wholesome general regulations." We should give "its full scope" to agriculture "in those states where people are fewer, tillage much more profitable, and provision dearer," and force manufactures only where soil is infertile, the industrious poor are to be found, and food is cheap. In South Carolina manufacture would entail "an evident loss—domestic manufacturing must be always excepted"; in Massachusetts "the advancement of that business" will give "means of subsistence to many." A liberal policy should insure that the produce of the Southern States is "exchanged for such manufactures as can be made by the Northern, free from duty." [57]

He proceeds to draw a picture in prospect of our country as it would "exist under the operation of a system of national laws formed upon these principles." In the foreground we should discover "the mass of our citizens—the cultivators—the independent proprietors of the soil." On one side we should see "our manufacturers encouraging the tillers of the earth" with their employment of the "fruits of their labors," and supplying "the rest of their fellow citizens with the instruments of their

occupations and the necessities and conveniences of life."
On the other, foreign commerce, "attentive to the general interest," would come forward "with offers to range through foreign climates," in search of supplies "which nature had not given at home and the manufacturer could not provide and to send in return the surplus of stores drawn from the ocean or produced by the earth."

In the attainment of such an economy the agency of the several states was not sufficient. Their acts proceed "on no uniform or permanent principles"; they undo in one year "those made in the preceding year" and clash "with the laws of other states"; they can "no longer be supported if we continue to be one people." Our commerce is more harassed "by the distractions and evils arising from the uncertainty, opposition, and errors of our trade laws than by the restrictions of any one power in Europe." A system which *"will promote the general interests, with the smallest injury to particular ones, has become indispensably necessary."* Accordingly the Congress should be enabled "to prevent every regulation that might oppose the general interest," and to restrict "the states from impolitic laws." It would be "perfectly safe" and of "excellent effect" to grant to the Congress "a negative upon all commercial acts of the legislatures." Such a measure would "gradually bring our national commercial system to order and perfection." [58]

As before, so after the event, a contemporary gloss continued to be written upon the text. Thomas Jefferson was not a member of the Convention. In creed and disposition he was not in full accord with all that was written into the Constitution. His chance officially to interpret the Constitution [59] did not come until he became Secretary of State at the inauguration of the new government. In the first year of the Republic, he forwarded to the House of Representatives a "petition of Boston sailmakers asking exclusive privilege of using particular marks" for designing sail cloth. The issue was of immediate concern with foreign commerce; but Jefferson had in mind the pristine use of trademarks to enable the consumer to trace defective wares to their makers and wanted to see the practice extended. In the course of his official communication he drew a distinction between "manufactures made and consumed within a state" which were "subject to state legislation" and "those which are exported to foreign nations, or to another state, or into the Indian territory" which "are, alone, within the jurisdiction of the General Government." [60]

If Thomas Jefferson had not been at the Convention, Alexander Hamilton had. He was well versed in all the intendments of the signers. In a *Report on Manufactures*,[61] as a good mercantilist he set himself to round out and improve the economy of the new republic. The distinctive geographical conditions—as well as the republican institutions—made it necessary to depart from the mercantilist scheme as it had been elaborated in Spain,

Portugal, France, and England. The United States possessed, in lieu of overseas colonies, vast territories to the west; legislative measures were to be shaped directly towards "enlarging the sphere of our domestic commerce." [62] So, in the mercantilist pattern, new-world style, the manufactures of England were to be replaced with those of the Seaboard, and States to be carved out of the wilderness were to supply raw materials. But, for all its accommodations to an expanding country, the lines of commercial policy stood out sharply.

In essence the document is a restatement—and an adaptation to American conditions—of the accepted body of mercantilist doctrine.[63] The means proper to its realization are:

> "1. Protecting duties . . . on those foreign articles which are the rivals of the domestic ones intended to be encouraged.
> "2. Prohibitions of rival articles, or duties equivalent to prohibitions.[64]
> "3. Prohibitions of the exportation of the materials of manufacturers.[65]
> "4. Pecuniary bounties.[66]
> "5. Premiums.
> "6. Exemptions of the materials of manufacture from duty.
> "7. Drawbacks of duties which are imposed on materials of manufacture.

"8. The encouragement of new inventions.

"9. Judicious regulations for the inspection of manufactured commodities.

"10. The facilitating of pecuniary remittances from place to place.[67]

"11. The facilitating of the transportation of commodities." [68]

As yet powers had been so little distinguished that a number of Hamilton's proposals for the encouragement of manufacture are to be achieved through the regulation of foreign commerce. The end is an American economy; the immediate objective is the encouragement of manufacture; the instrument is the regulation of foreign commerce. In the thought of the day it was an obvious way to think of manufacture and a natural approach to the problem of production.[69]

The *Report on Manufactures* was no isolated document. It was meant to clarify and direct national policy. It emerged from the concern of the new government with problems of state. In his first speech to the Congress, President Washington had said, "The advancement of agriculture, commerce, and manufactures by all proper means, will not, I trust, need recommendation." The House of Representatives, the Senate in accord, had answered. "We concur with you in the sentiment that 'agriculture, commerce and manufactures' are entitled to legislative protection." [70]

All of this—memorandum and broadside, pamphlet and polemic—is the babble of many voices. Yet they speak in a single tongue. In 1791 the living words of the Constitution—not yet stereotyped into rigid verbal symbol—were still broad enough to meet the exigencies of the moment and to allow a national attack upon a problem of the general welfare.

Interests are the elements of the commonwealth. The office of the general government is to nurture and guard them. A congressional regulation of all that is commerce is alike an instrument of national defense and a source of national opulence.

Here is the pattern of competitive nationalism—the application of a political economy—the ways of the mind in the Eighteenth Century.

4. The Writing on Parchment

As is fitting with an instrument designed to establish a government, a preamble begins the Constitution. It was written last and expresses in clean-cut infinitives the great tasks of state which the signers had come to set down for the new republic. The narrow pedantry of a later age has affected to regard the opening statement as no part of the Constitution, and to set it aside as a glorified flourish to a legalistic document. But it is an expression of the very spirit of the Convention.[71] Its injunctions "to form a more perfect Union," "to establish Justice," "to promote domestic Tranquility," "to secure the Blessings of Liberty to ourselves and our Posterity," and "to promote the general Welfare" are criteria of public policy. In a society in which "essential principles ought to be accommodated to time and place" they are standards of reference in the continuous application of the detailed provisions to the affairs of the nation. Without such a guide constitutional interpretation falls a prey to the letter of the law that kills.[72]

The document itself falls into three related parts. There is, first, a provision of arrangements for a federal state; next, a division of powers between national and state authority; and last—largely in the Ten Amendments added to secure ratification—a statement of the limits of the province of government. Even the framework is only a structure about which the usages of a living government might grow up. Nowhere, in the sections which have to do with powers and policies, is there a categorical imperative. The constitutional provisions are elastic formulas, adequate to the infinite variety of the changing circumstances of national life.[73] Their general terms are to be filled with the factual evidence of the occasion, and the decision is to go where the balance of values lies. An absence of specific command and detailed prohibition gives to a document from the later Eighteenth Century a relative immortality.

The touch of the same creative restraint marks the grant of powers to the Congress. Although the Fathers were mercantilists, they imposed little restraint upon the authority they created. Manufacturers are to be encouraged, export duties are not to be laid upon staples, the slave trade is to have a limited protection. But such indulgence in policy-making does not go far. The authors of the Supreme law had an everyday familiarity with regulation; they did not shudder at the idea of power—provided it was, by a shrewd system of elections, lodged with the wise and the good. Staunch in their own faith, they were content to grant a broad authority and to allow the Congress to accommodate measures to passing events.[74]

It is significant that powers are enumerated but never defined. A trade might pass over from the domestic to the moneyed economy; a commerce local in character might come to be among the several states. A commercial revolution, with its contribution to the opulence of nations, was a matter of common knowledge. An industrial revolution—though the term still lay some decades in the future—was well under way in England. Out of it new inventions, strange problems, unfamiliar ways of thought, and an alien culture were destined to come. On the eve of changes which could be sensed, even if not foreseen in detail, it would have been short-sighted to reduce powers to bills of particulars. It would have been folly to distribute for all time between nation and states aspects of a culture in process of transformation.[75] Such a procedure would have invited a dynamic economic order to shape its growth to the grooves of a rigid legal system.[76]

Nor did strict definition serve even current necessity. The task of the delegates was to establish a nation which was yet far from a going concern. Independence had been won but not yet made secure. The peace with England was, as later events revealed, a truce that might be broken at any time. The friendship with France could not survive a trend towards revolution already in evidence. The tumultuous unrest of all Europe was still to spend itself in the Napoleonic drama. A group of rival nations fought each other with armies and blockades, alliances and tariffs; and, when peace came, the spirit of war found vent in commercial policy. Among the hostile and jealous nations of the world the new republic had to win its place. It had to protect itself against their aggressions; to free its trade and government from dependence upon foreign powers it could not trust. The task ahead was not to be accomplished by the niggardly use of a few paltry powers; it demanded—after the manner of the times—authority to shape an economy into a bulwark for the nation.

Accordingly, to the Fathers the "grants" were not so many distinct powers, each with its separate domain and specified use. Instead they were so many weapons which might be used singly or in concert as political occasion demanded. The broadest of all was the war power.[77] Inseparable from the authority to impose taxes and to regulate commerce, it might conscript other powers to its use;[78] for, in the Eighteenth Century, war as fully as peace was the normal state of the nation. For purposes of national defense the powers over commerce and over taxation were complements: the one marked out a domain of regulation, the other supplied the directing instrument. The tax power might be employed to wring from another state a favorable balance of trade. The treaty power might be used in shaping the commercial system of the nation. Or, in a more advanced policy, a tax on imports, imposed in the spirit of war, might induce a foreign state to enter into a treaty designed to regulate commerce. The power "to coin money and fix the value thereof" was as comprehensive as the pecuniary means of exchange of the times.[79] And, as lesser devices, there was the granting of patents and the regulation of bankruptcies. Here was an arsenal, equipped with all the techniques essential to the power to govern. All such powers were part and parcel of the national authority over commerce.[80]

A narrowing of the concept "commerce" is at odds with contemporary usage. If the Fathers intended to exclude from the term regulation of overseas trade, buying and selling within the internal economy, the encouragement of manufacture—or even activities which reach out towards cultural usages—the records will be sought in vain for such restriction. If they intended the same word, in each of its references—to foreign trade, among the several states, and with the Indian tribes—to be used in a different sense, they left no glossary to tell expositors how narrow or how wide to carve the domains.[81] The general correspondence of the commercial provisions in the Constitution with the Acts of Trade and Navigation of Great Britain is too striking to be escaped. A different national economy is the objective; but the policy of regulation and the devices it employs bear the distinctive mark of the mercantile century.

The spirit of its creators is the mark of the document. The Fathers hoped the government they were creating would endure. They knew they could not foresee the course of human events which stretched ahead. They made no attempt to anticipate every problem, to meet every contingency, to guard against every danger of future national life. They wrote no intricate body of rules abstractly suited to the detailed exigencies of situations unknown; they set down no involved code of general principles, smothered beneath qualifications and exceptions, for meeting future national emergencies. They created no august and inflexible corpus of constitutional law.

Instead they wrote the briefest sort of a document. They laid down a structure for a state and endowed the Federal Government with the most general powers. In all their lines they employed short clauses made of broad words of general import. They were concerned to list matters of national importance and to point the direction for public policy. They were content to leave its detailed formulation to their descendants who would be better able to shape remedies to their own necessities. In this declaration of political faith in posterity they created a purposive and flexible instrument which allowed a gracious accommodation of government to the changing needs of future decades.

In its detail of provisions the same clear note of directness is in evidence. The Framers were themselves trying to escape an inflexible constitution; they were much too wise to impose an iron-clad code on their descendants. They saw too keenly how the understanding of a former generation had failed to solve current problems to be at all certain of their own ability to answer questions which could not be asked for years to come. It was impossible for them to escape the values, opinions, and beliefs of the later Eighteenth Century. But, as men who accounted themselves products of the Age of Reason, their eyes took in the distant scene.

The intent of the Fathers was to establish in the broadest of terms a living instrument of government—not to garner ritualistic rules of political conduct into a rigid code. The Constitution was a charter for a new republic destined in time to meet all the vicissitudes of national existence.

· VII ·

The Voice of Another Age

SEVENTEEN EIGHTY-SEVEN is a long time ago. It goes without saying that the Constitution which emerged from the Convention at Philadelphia is not—and ought not to be—the Constitution of today.

In the current world it would be impossible to endow the classic lines with the content and significance it had for the signers. The meaning of words, the quality of opinion, the state of knowledge, the industrial problems which are current, the ends of public policy, have all changed beyond recognition. It is beyond the power of the jurist who is most scrupulous in regard to his oath to make it live again with the breath of an age that is gone. To bring to a current interpretation of "the supreme law of the land" the meanings of words, the common sense of the departed economy, the political aspirations of a far-off era, would be as unthinkable as it would prove confusing.

We are no longer concerned to impose a mercantile pattern on our national economy. The primacy of such questions as the encouragement of manufacture, the barrier against paper money, and the use of compacts and arms to bring foreign power to terms is broken. The agricultural and the commercial interests are no longer the exclusive parties to the state. The system of election which reserved public office to gentlemen has survived only as a formality. The tenant farmer, the industrial worker, the women who work, have all come into the body politic. An extension of suffrage has made their mills articulate. They have brought to public policy a host of new problems of which the Fathers never dreamed—the protection of hours and wages against the havoc of an overdone competition, the security of life against the grosser hazards of unemployment and dependency in old age, the domestication of an unruly industrial system to the humanity it should serve.

In the Constitution of 1787 there is nothing adamant to such demands of an awakening democracy. The newer public control may employ different techniques and serve a new master, but it accommodates itself easily to an instrument of government so framed that there might be power to regulate and advance the wealth of the nation. In spite of general provisions—free from categorical detail—the Fathers hardly hoped that their instrument would endure. Its survival against the impact of a century and a half of tumultuous events proclaims the receptivity of its provisions to changing winds of doctrine and ever-new definitions of national destiny. Its vitality lies in its allowance of leeway, in its provision for interstitial growth, in an eventual accommodation of provision to major circumstance. It is, as a living thing, a tissue of changing usages, established about a general outline, and drawing sanctions from the writing on parchment.

Its current inadequacy flows from the gloss. As mercantilism passed, into the intellectual succession then came—along with the machine, the corporation, and business—another economic philosophy. In the articles of faith which is *laissez-faire*, business is more capable than the state to encourage manufacture, to regulate industry, and to direct the activities of the people toward prosperity. The government is the villain in the piece, and the frontiers of Business Enterprise must be protected against its encroachments. Another route led to the general welfare.

All through the Nineteenth Century this outlook upon affairs gained ground. It made its appeal to the mind of man, reduced a virile political economy to a body of dogma, and came to dominate public policy. It is a truth self-evident to persons who wish to be left to their own devices; it is entrenched behind strong emotional defenses; its appeal reaches down to the very foundations of human preference. It is a part of a general outlook, an aspect of an intellectual atmosphere in which men live. It pervades the prevailing disciplines of the intellect and gets itself tangled into the scheme of values by which men and judges reach decisions. Its sanctions are

more compelling than a barrage of precedents; its usages
are more insistent than cold logic or the icy march of
argument.

It had already permeated common sense, economic
theory, and public policy. It would have been strange
if it had not made its way into constitutional interpretation. It was borne along on the current of the age, and
had behind it the dominant interest that sought to become vested. The supreme law of the land was not
immune to an outlook on affairs which had already
penetrated the infringing intellectual world. In the process, the terms of old legal formulas were filled with the
wish fulfillments of industrialists and made to live with
the ingenious inventions of lawyers. As expediency
would have it, the "due process" clause of the Fourteenth
Amendment was first touched; it was, through a series
of interpretations, made into the likeness of the economic
theory of *laissez-faire*. In time, the "due process" clause
of the Fifth Amendment was reanimated with the borrowed exegesis. A belated interpretation has conferred
upon the corporation, as a barrier against social legislation, the rights of man. And privileges conferred upon
its creature by the state have become rights against the
creator.

Into the judicial drama the commerce clause was
drawn. In their growth industries had exhibited a negli-
gence of state lines; matters calling for correction were
beyond the competence of the states; the Federal Gov-

ernment was sought as an agency of regulation. In appeals to the Court the Tenth Amendment was invoked; the attorneys for corporations exhibited a new and deep solicitude for the vanishing rights of the states; and the commerce clause was subjected to surgical scrutiny. A novel way of the mind was applied in interpretation; and an attempt was made to resolve in the two distinct categories of "federal" and "state" a miscellany of activities tangled together into an organic economic system. A physical analogy was invoked to help the novel cause along. There emerged a new verbal craft for measuring legislation against the commerce clause. Commerce was "stream" or "flow." It did or did not "move" or "cut across" state boundaries. If it did the Federal Government might remove "burdens" upon it or "obstacles" to it. That a line—which severed things that were inseparable—might be accurately drawn, meticulous attention had to be given to a separation of the "direct" from the "indirect" effects of the actions of the government upon "the stream of commerce." [1] To many of its skilled practitioners this verbal symbolism became the reality of commerce.

But the Constitution yields decorously. The invasion of its texture by the doctrine of *laissez-faire* was a slow process. It was long after the power over commerce had bowed to the dominant political opinion before the power to tax began to be stripped of its regulatory authority.[2] It was not until 1936 that it was belatedly held that its use must have a relevant connection with some specific power entrusted by the people to the Congress.[3] A beginning has just been made of the argument that the Federal Government has no power to engage in business in competition with its own citizens. As yet the spending power is quite untouched by the economic philosophy of "do-nothing." The judicial chapter did not start until the whirl of industrialism had put *laissez-faire* on the defensive; its recent victories have been won with its popular cause in full retreat.

It is the event which matters; the detail is of the lesser importance. It was easy enough to find legal henchmen who could be furbished out in the newer constitutional trappings to protect the frontiers of business enterprise against government interference. The ingenuity shown is startlingly evident in the renaissance of the legal doctrine of states' rights where no rights of the state are involved.[4] But constitutional rhetoric must be on its good behavior. When the choice is between federal regulation or an absence of control, the fiction of the right of sovereign states serves its pragmatic purpose.

The undeniable urge toward writing the theory of individualism into the Constitution makes use of the most tractable materials at hand. It might easily have found expression in a very different system of constitutional law. But it was too powerful, and too fully in accord with the way the country was tending, to be denied. The urge was persistent; the technical task was to correlate the newer objectives with the older values of the document. In this work the majority of the Supreme Court has exhibited dialectic talents of high order. It has made a none too tractable instrument of government, dating from the Eighteenth Century, reflect the opinion of its own intellectual world.

A number of bothers have attended its coming. It has made the judicial expression of the voice of the people the voice of a small and unrepresentative minority. It has brought to judgment upon public policy all the attitudes, techniques, and procedures of private law. It has left final discretion upon the limits of the province of government to a small professional group whose competence is not primarily in matters of policy and the realities of the industrial world. It has confused the formulation and execution of programs of legislation with protracted periods of paralyzing uncertainty.

It has, above all, come into constitutional law far too late. The usage of declaring an act void in the name of the Constitution has a respectable lineage; its reference to *laissez-faire* as a standard of validity is new. It was not until the late eighties that "due process of law" won judicial acceptance as a challenge to legislation; and when, in the classic "bakeshop case," [5] it was set down in dissent that "the Constitution does not embody a particular economic theory, whether of individualism or of paternalism," Mr. Justice Holmes was fighting a rearguard action, [6] not attempting to capture a new salient.

And long before the creed of *laissez-faire* had come into judicial ascendancy, it had been challenged and was losing ground as an aspect of common sense, political opinion, and public policy. In fact it was the very expression of the still more recent philosophy of public control in legislation [7] which imposed upon the courts the role of defender of the nineteenth-century faith 'of *laissez-faire*.

The result has been the creation of an anomalous situation. It is as true as ever it was that the power to regulate commerce "among the states" belongs to the federal and "within a state" to the state government. The law and the categories remained fixed. The issue has been shifted from the major premise of law to the minor premise of fact. The question has become what commerce is "national" and what is "local" in character. Upon that question the citation of precedents and the enumeration of instances can throw little light. In the dynamic swing into the future such things as techniques, business methods, and markets refuse to abide; and industries change their character with the march of the years. The law is clear enough, but as case follows case the facts must be freshly appraised.

An unending industrial revolution separates now from the then of 1787. The domestic trades have left the home; about each an industry has been established; and industries have been loosely agglomerated into an economic order. In its growth the economic order has paid little attention to state boundaries; its far-flung lines are integrated into an organic whole; the forces which give or withhold employment record the residual item of the balance-sheet in black or red, and bring the alternation of prosperity or depression, come, literally, from the ends of an industrial system more than national in its reach. As the decades have passed—in terms of sheer undisputed fact—item after item has passed from the domestic to the commercial economy, or from a commerce within a state to a commerce among the several states. To hold objects within the regulating authority to which once they belonged, is to overlook the plain words of the Constitution. It is a surrender to the individual states of the regulation of a "commerce among the several states." It is an injunction alike to deny current fact and to pervert constitutional law. If an application of the commerce clause as it was plainly written [8] narrows the province of state regulation, it is the industrial system which is to blame. It has ceased to be local in character. Affairs of commerce have emerged in which the several states lack competence. And it has come about without conscious intent [9] on the part of anyone.

Here lies a most ingenious paradox. As industry has become more and more interstate in character, the power of Congress to regulate has been given a narrower and narrower interpretation. The novelties in judicial doctrine cannot be explained as a belated anxiety for the police power of the states, for state acts have been stricken down as freely as federal. Nor are the litigants who appeal to the courts against the legislature unusually solicitous about the preservation of the integrity of the power of the states. The Tenth Amendment is to them a convenient device by which the frontiers of the business system may be protected against invasion. The strong urge which has of late impelled conscientious justices to a sincere disapproval of Acts of Congress is a deep-seated distrust of the capacity of the Federal Government to give orders, direction, and purpose to the affairs of business.

At the moment the issue is exciting because of the clash of social philosophies. If the doctrine of *laissez-faire* were in its heyday, or if the idea of a social control of business were still a chimera, a living Constitution might reflect a universally accepted public policy. But an older common sense has it that the interference of the government can bring only paralysis and confusion into the affairs of business. And a newer common sense declares that industry lacks the capacity for self-government; that regulation lies beyond the state's competence; and that the only choice is between Federal control and chaos.[10] A constitution which was an embodiment of mercantilist doctrine has become an expression of the creed of economic individualism. An instrument so yielding to insistent pressures is flexible enough to meet the democratic demands of the immediate future.

The abiding text can again be furbished out with a more fitting gloss.

A conflict persists within the government. The Congress, dominated by a national democracy, is intent upon a program of social legislation. The judiciary, representing a powerful minority, would hold a government which is not to be trusted to a restricted regulatory sphere. If policy is to go its public way, the conflict must be resolved. There may for a time be delay, confusion, or sham battle; but the course of events which hurries the nation towards an unknown future will not be long stayed by even the most conscientious judicial scruples.

The issue may be deferred; it cannot be escaped. It may be that presently jurists will be able to spell out the text of the Constitution beneath the miscellany of comment from the bench. It may be that Legislature and Executive, exercising their constitutional powers, will contrive ways and means for drawing erring judicial eyes from the margin back to the page. It may be that the gloss lies so thick that the power to govern must be written afresh in the language of today.

No matter. . . . A great democracy can be depended upon to make of the Constitution a living instrument of government. Grooves can never be cut for the destiny of a nation.

Notes on the Text

CHAPTER I

1. It is, of course, clear to the reader that "the political state" and "the economic order" are terms of verbal shorthand that comprehend a miscellany of particulars. They are not entities outside of and above society, but names for established ways through which the persons and interests that make up a community act.

2. The word "industry" is used for the dominant opinion of the business community. The term is recent; it was established before the depression; the National Industrial Recovery Administration made its use all but universal.

3. *Panama Refining Co. v. Ryan*, 293 U.S. 388 (1935).

4. In *Norman v. Baltimore and Ohio R. R. Co.*, 294 U.S. 240 (1935), the action of the government was approved in respect to private contracts.

5. *Railroad Retirement Board v. Alton*, 295 U.S. 330 (1935). The act provided, among other things, for assessments upon railroad companies, to be paid into a fund out of which retirement allowances were to be paid. This arrangement for pooling disturbed a majority of the Court who were disposed to view it as a taking of property without due process of law.

6. *Schechter Corp. v. U. S.*, 295 U.S. 495 (1935). It was also held that the administrative structure of the National Industrial Recovery Administration was wanting in a proper delegation of power to the executive.

7. *U. S. v. Butler*, 297 U.S. 1 (1936).

8. *Ashwander v. Tennessee Valley Authority*, 297 U.S. 288 (1936).

9. It is curious to know—we shall probably never find out—just what deliberation lies back of the TVA decision. It followed immediately after the great storm of criticism in the press, and in Congress,

raised by the AAA decision; and it was—for a New Deal case—
before the Court an unusually long time. Not one of the many
distinguished legal prophets was able to predict in advance just what
the decision was to be. The case was disposed of by a most unusual
series of votes. First, the Chief Justice joined with the four "stal-
warts" to find a minority stockholder entitled to a cause of action
in respect to a contract entered into by his corporation. Then Mr.
Justice McReynolds withdrew, to leave the Chief Justice, Mr. Justice
Van Devanter, Mr. Justice Sutherland, and Mr. Justice Butler to
declare that the legislation was a proper exercise of federal powers
for war and over navigation, and that the production and sale of
electrical energy was valid as to these powers.

In the result—but not in this argument—Mr. Justice Brandeis, Mr.
Justice Stone, Mr. Justice Roberts, and Mr. Justice Cardozo joined.
Their argument, voiced by Mr. Justice Brandeis, was only to the
effect that the minority stockholder had no rightful cause of action
and the Court had no jurisdiction. Thus, if a rule of substantive law
is to be found in the case, it is to be discovered in the statement
by Mr. Chief Justice Hughes, which had the support of Mr. Justice
McReynolds dissenting.

It is easy enough to set down half-a-dozen equally plausible ways
in which the case might have been disposed of. It is no wonder that
a number of keen judicial observers believe that the Chief Justice,
stung by the criticism of the Court after the AAA decision, set
about winning back for the august tribunal its reputation for judicial
impartiality; and in this decision, which allows a victory to the government without any violence to the *laissez-faire* of his conservative
colleagues, executed a superb judicial maneuver. In any event the
result was decisive, eight Justices concurring, and only Mr. Justice
McReynolds dissenting.

10. *Carter v. Carter Coal Co.*, 298 U.S. 238 (1936).

11. The Bituminous Coal Conservation Act of 1935, C. 824, 49
Stat. 991.

12. A distinctive feature was a device for the protection of the
consumer. The office of the Consumers' Counsel was established
independently of the Commission, and was endowed with powers
to investigate, to subpoena witnesses, to publish findings, and to
report to Congress.

13. *Carter v. Carter Coal Co.* and *Carter v. Helvering*, 12 F. S. 570.

14. *R. C. Tway Coal Co. v. Glenn*, 12 F. S. 570.

15. The Court recognized the "considerations" which impelled Congress to pass the act: viz., to protect the general interest, health, and comfort of the people, to conserve privately-owned coal, to maintain just relations between producers and employees and others, and to promote the general welfare, by controlling nation-wide production and distribution of coal. "These," said the Court, "it may be conceded, are objects of great worth; but are they ends, the attainment of which has been committed by the Constitution to the Federal Government?" *Loc. cit.*, at pp. 290-291.

16. Mr. Justice Van Devanter, Mr. Justice McReynolds, Mr. Justice Butler, and Mr. Justice Roberts concurred with Mr. Justice Sutherland. Mr. Justice Cardozo dissented in an opinion in which Mr. Justice Brandeis and Mr. Justice Stone joined. It is generally assumed that the separate opinion of Mr. Chief Justice Hughes is a dissent, but with strict accuracy it can be described neither as concurrence nor dissent.

17. The stress of Mr. Justice Cardozo's dissent falls upon the severability of the labor provisions. Although it is legal in its terms, its logic is realistic. For with a union strong enough to enforce collective bargaining throughout the industry, there is, quite apart from the state, an agency of control which is adequate to fix wages, regulate hours, and establish minimum labor standards. The invocation of the state is necessary only to regulate output, establish fair prices, and check the untoward effects of an overdone competition.

18. It is of note that the majority and minority of the Court failed to meet upon the issues. The majority refused to say that the price-fixing provisions were in themselves invalid; the minority did not argue that the labor provisions were valid.

19. *Stafford v. Wallace*, 258 U.S. 495 (1922).

20. *Board of Trade v. Olsen*, 262 U.S. 1 (1923). See also *Lemke v. Farmers' Grain Co.*, 258 U.S. 50 (1922).

21. *Loewe v. Lawlor*, 208 U.S. 274 (1908); *Duplex Printing Press Co. v. Deering*, 254 U.S. 443 (1921); *U. S. v. Brimms*, 272 U.S. 549 (1926); *Bedford Cut-Stone Co. v. Journeymen Stone-Cutters' Ass'n*, 274 U.S. 37 (1927).

22. *Appalachian Coals Case*, 288 U.S. 344 (1933). For a full discussion of these cases see Corwin, E. S., *The Commerce Power v. States Rights*, 1936, pp. 189-209.

23. *Carter v. Carter Coal Co.*, *loc. cit.*, at p. 298.

24. *Ibid.*, at p. 303.

25. *Ibid.*, at pp. 308-309.

26. *Kidd v. Pearson*, 128 U.S. 1 (1888).

27. *U. S. v. E. C. Knight*, 156 U.S. 1 (1895), at p. 12.

28. *Oliver Iron Co. v. Lord*, 262 U.S. 172 (1923), at p. 179.

29. *Schechter Corp. v. U. S.*, *loc. cit.*

30. *Utah Power and Light Co. v. Pfost*, 286 U.S. 165 (1932), at p. 551.

31. To establish the intrinsic local character of production, Mr. Justice Sutherland also cites *Chassaniol v. Greenwood*, 291 U. S. 584 (1934).

32. *Carter v. Carter Coal Co.*, *loc. cit.*, at p. 303.

33. Almost on the heels of the Carter case came the decision of the Court in *Morehead v. New York ex rel. Tipaldo*, 298 U.S. 587 (1936), outlawing the act of the State of New York providing for a minimum wage for women in industry. In this judgment the provisions of the act were found to be a taking of property without due process of law in contravention of the Fourteenth Amendment. The press and public were shocked to discover how forgetful the Court had become of the police power for the states, a professed solicitude for which prompted the decision in the Carter case.

CHAPTER II

1. Schlesinger, A. M., *The Colonial Merchants and the American Revolution, 1763-1776.*

2. Since the economy of the country rested squarely upon small agricultural units this was not necessarily a disaster of the first magnitude to the nation as a whole, but it bore heavily upon men of affairs.

3. Anderson, Adam, *An Historical and Chronological Deduction of the Origin of Commerce.* London, 1787, p. lxii.

4. Nevins, Allan, *The American States During and After the Revolution, 1775-1789* (1924), *passim;* Jameson, J. Franklin, *The American Revolution Considered as a Social Movement*, 1926.

5. Nevins, pp. 507-572.

6. Nevins, ch. 12, pp. 544-605.

7. An historically accurate account of the rebellion is to be found in Edward Bellamy's *The Duke of Stockbridge*.

8. Madison, *Writings* (Hunt ed.), II, pp. 260-262.

9. See for example the circular of the Boston merchants of 1788 "to their brethren in the several seaports of the Union." Winsor, Justin, *Memorial History of Boston*, Vol. IV, Chap. III; cf. *Magazine of American History*, April, 1893, p. 324 ff.; *American Museum*, Vol. I, chapter on American manufactures. Beard discusses this consciousness of identity of interest shown by the commercial class in *An Economic Interpretation of the Constitution of the U. S.*, 1935, pp. 40-49.

10. Elliot, Jonathan, *The Debates in the Several State Conventions on the Adoption of the Federal Constitution . . . together with the Journal of the Federal Convention . . . Virginia and Kentucky Resolutions and other Illustrations of the Constitution*, 1836, Vol. I, p. 92.

11. *Ibid.*, pp. 106-108. The report is concerned wholly with foreign commerce, the situation of which affected the fortune of every citizen, for "it is the constant source of wealth and incentive to industry; and the value of our produce and our land must ever rise or fall in proportion to the prosperous or adverse state of trade."
    After noticing the "unenlightened" British measures it states, "unless the United States in Congress assembled shall be vested with powers competent to the protection of commerce, they can never command reciprocal advantages in trade; and without these our foreign commerce must decline and eventually be annihilated."

12. The Virginia Resolution is given in Elliot, p. 108; see *American Museum*, Vol. I, p. 313 (quoted in Beard, p. 41) for the Pennsylvania memorial.

13. Elliot, p. 115.

14. Beginning in 1782, Congress with increasing insistence asked the states to grant power to lay a five percent duty on all foreign imports, to be collected by Congressional customs officers. The power so vested was to be limited in duration and all revenues accumulated were to be applied to the existing national debt. Although all the states but Rhode Island agreed to the proposal in principle the necessary enabling legislation was not passed. In 1786 seven states only had taken real action; three states had passed laws "so inconsonant with the spirit of the plan" that they "could not be deemed compliances"; and three states had taken no action whatsoever.

15. Elliot, p. 118.

16. Careful students of American history have debated for years the question of the "critical" situation of the Union in 1787. Many citizens had no inkling that they were living in the midst of anarchy and that chaos threatened to engulf them. See Dawson, H. B., *The Historical Magazine*, 1871, Vol. IX, pp. 157 ff. It cannot be doubted, however, that men in all sections, including leaders such as Washington and Madison, whose patriotism and disinterested statesmanship cannot be questioned, believed that a continuance of the commercial disorders and state quarrels presaged inevitable dissolution of the Confederation and possibly conquest by European powers. See Warren, Charles, *The Making of the Constitution*, 1928, Ch. II.

That the business depression was unusually severe is also questionable. Franklin, in the winter of 1787, stated that the country, on the whole, was so prosperous that there was every reason for profound thanksgiving. He admitted that there were some who complained of hard times, slack trade, and scarcity of money, but he added that there never was an age nor a country in which there were not some people so circumstanced as to find it hard to make a living and that "it is always in the power of a small number to make a great clamour." But viewing the several classes in the community as a whole, prosperity, contended Franklin, was widespread and obvious. Never was the farmer paid better for his products, "as the published prices current abundantly testify. The lands he possesses are continually rising in value. In no part of Europe are the labouring poor so well paid, fed, or clothed." The fishing trade, he thinks, is in a rather bad way, and mercantile branches are overcrowded; but he is not distressed by the extensive importation of English goods because this is nothing new, and America has prospered in spite of it. M. Carey, *The American Museum*, January, 1787, Vol. I, pp. 5 ff. quoted in Beard, p. 48.

17. From Madison's rough draft of a preface for his notes on the Debates in the Convention. The full text is printed in Farrand, Max, *The Records of the Federal Convention of 1787* (1934), Vol. III, pp. 539-551.

18. There were, of course, jibes at the talk of hard times. A Virginian essayist, in a *Proof of the Scarcity of Money*, states that this scarcity so hampered racing during the year that ten tracks in the state paid only £2,610 to winners. Great crowds of poverty-stricken people, in fine clothes, thronged to the meets to bet, and

now only five times as many drove up in four-wheeled carriages as did two decades past. Owners of winning cocks in the local pits were greatly distressed because they received only £355 in prizes; and it was indeed pitiable to see the audiences of penniless men, who, eager to forget their money troubles, crowded the Richmond and Petersburg theaters to suffocation. (*New Haven Gazette*, October 5, 1786. Quoted in Nevins, p. 518.)

19. George Washington, *To the Congress, In Convention*, September 17, 1787. The objection to "one body of men" was to the repository of the powers of the Confederation, such as they were, in the Congress alone. Under the Constitution there came to be three departments of government with a "separation of powers."

20. Farrand, I, p. 405; II, pp. 3, 648.

21. The term Fathers is technical. Its more usual meaning is "the signers of the Constitution"; but it also habitually refers to the body of delegates who sat in the Convention. It signifies nothing about the age of the persons it describes; and its etymological significance has been lost.

22. The men who had been most active in the Confederation in pressing for the regulation of commerce were in the Convention. Hamilton, Madison, and Fitzsimmons had been exponents of the five percent Congressional impost. When Rhode Island protested, it was Madison, Hamilton, and Ellsworth who drew up the official answer. In 1784, Pinckney and Gorham had been among those who sought commercial advantage with foreign nations through a navigation act. And four of the five members of the Committee on Commerce of 1785—Spaight of North Carolina, Houston of Georgia, Johnson of Connecticut, and King of Massachusetts—two years later became delegates to the Convention.

23. In spite of the prominent part played by lawyers in the Revolution, at its close the profession had fallen in quality and esteem. Many of the distinguished older members of the bar had been evicted with the Tories; the most brilliant young men, like Hamilton, were deeply involved in politics; the social and financial unrest had cast the stigma of oppressor upon the men of low grade and inferior abilities who sought to enforce contracts and filled the debtor prisons. Moreover dozens of local statutes were passed "to regulate the profession." The law regained its prestige as the profession revived and as the stigma of "un-American" was removed from the English com-

mon law by native annotators who gave it a strangely "republican" twist. For an excellent example of this see St. George Tucker's edition of Blackstone's *Commentaries*.

24. In *An Economic Interpretation of the Constitution*, Charles A. Beard showed that the Fathers were, as a group, "rich and well born" and that most of them benefited financially from the formation of the national government. The storm of protest, loosed by critics of this work, has offered nothing to controvert the facts. Madison's preface to the debates is as much of an economic interpretation to the Constitution as anything Beard has written.

25. Richard Henry Lee in a pamphlet criticizing certain features of the Constitution, which Vernon Parrington (*Main Currents in American Thought*, Vol. I, p. 290) feels comes nearest to being a "frank and disinterested examination of the proposed instrument," considered it "a very unfortunate event" that the Convention, as it finally met, contained so many men "principally connected with commerce and the judicial departments." If the "many good republican characters" such as Patrick Henry (who refused to attend because he "smelt a Rat") had been present, Lee felt that the result ". . . would not have had that strong tendency to aristocracy now discernible in every part of the plan," and "the young visionary men, and the consolidating aristocracy would have been more restrained than they have been."

CHAPTER III

1. Note particularly the dictionaries of Dr. Samuel Johnson. A great deal that has been charged to his personal eccentricity has at least a basis in current lexicographic usage.

As yet the dictionaries had not obtained objectivity. They reflected the opinions of the authors—and of the age—upon the thing which the word sought to define. If such a practice impairs, it also enhances their usefulness today.

2. Mathews, Mitford McLeod, *A Survey of English Dictionaries*, 1933, devotes a chapter to the relative merits and demerits of the dictionaries of the Eighteenth Century.

3. The *Encyclopedia Britannica* notes that "the lexicographer was long expected to register only words deemed 'good' for literary use, with their proper meanings. It was his duty to sift and refine, to decide authoritatively questions of usage, and thus fix the language

as completely as might be possible within the limits determined by the literary taste of his time."

Johnson's dictionary was an attempt to do this. But the learned Doctor was not overly optimistic of his success. In the preface he states, "There is in constancy and stability a general and lasting advantage. . . . This recommendation of steadiness and uniformity does not proceed from an opinion that particular combinations of letters have much influence on human happiness, or that truth may not be taught by modes of spelling fanciful and erroneous. I am not yet so lost in lexicography, as to forget that *words are the daughters of earth and that things are the sons of heaven.* Language is only the instrument of science, and words are but the signs of ideas: I wish, however, that the instrument might be less apt to decay, and that the signs might be permanent, like the things which they denote." Johnson, Samuel, *A Dictionary of the English Language*, 1755.

4. As Johnson bluntly puts it, "That many terms of art and manufacture are omitted must be frankly acknowledged; but for this defect I may boldly allege that it was unavoidable: I could not visit caverns to learn the miner's language, nor take a voyage to perfect my skill in the dialect of navigation, nor visit the merchants, and . . . artificers to gain the names of wares, tools and operations, of which no mention is found in books. . . ."

5. For example see William Kenrick's *A New Dictionary of the English Language*, 1773, which offered not only "the Explanation of Words . . . but likewise their *Orthoepia,* or Pronunciation in Speech, according to the present Practice of Polished Speakers in the Metropolis."

6. William Rider, *A New Universal English Dictionary; or a Compleat Treasure of the English Language*, 1759.

7. James Barclay, *A Complete and Universal English Dictionary*, 1782. Page citation is not given as few of the dictionaries numbered the pages.

8. Nathan Bailey, *An Universal Etymological English Dictionary*, 1782.

9. Hogarth's attack on those "canting artists" who tried to cry up an art-for-art's-sake school in the last years of the century arises from this basic assumption. It is of note that the craft of portraiture reached its height in England during this period.

10. Bailey, Barclay.

11. John Marchant, *A New Complete English Dictionary*, 1760.

12. "A man who acts wholly at the command or the pleasure of another is called a *machine* among the dramatic poets." Dyche, Thomas, *A New General English Dictionary*, 1777.

13. Dyche.

14. The term seems first to have been used by W. S. Jevons in *The Coal Question*, 1866; it was popularized by Arnold Toynbee in *Lectures on the Industrial Revolution in England*, 1884.

15. Dr. Benjamin Franklin and Mr. Thomas Jefferson were only the most conspicuous among those who contributed to the progress of mechanical arts in Colonial America.

16. Barclay, Johnson, Marchant.

17. Barclay, *cf.* William Scott, *A New Spelling, Pronouncing, and Explanatory Dictionary of the English Language*, 1797; John Entick, *Entick's New Spelling Dictionary*, 1786.

18. An aristocratic lexicographer could not forego his chance to scoff; notice Samuel Johnson's quotation from Swift: "The profaneness and ignorance of handicraftsmen, small traders, servants, and the like, are to a degree very hard to be imagined greater."

19. Benjamin Martin, *Lingua Britannica Reformata, or a New Universal English Dictionary*, 1754; John Ash, *A New and Complete Dictionary of the English Language*, 1775; Kenrick.

20. Martin, Barclay.

21. Marchant, Dyche, Barclay, Rider, Martin.

22. Rider, Martin, Barclay, Bailey, Marchant.

23. *Vd., infra*, p. 81.

24. Although wealth, the state of well-being, had long since taken to itself other meanings, up to the Revolution those colonists who belonged to the established Church prayed for the "health and wealth" of King George. See *Book of Common Prayer*.

25. Dyche.

26. Dexter Keezer gives a history of the word in *Encyclopedia of Social Sciences;* see also the *Oxford English Dictionary*.

27. The examples cited in Johnson's dictionary reveal the wide

general range of the word; Kenrick offers a good picture of its more mundane and colloquial usage.

Barclay, with an erudite marvel of hair-fine distinction, stresses that: "*Business* implies an object of industry; *affairs* an object of concern. The first implies the hands; the second the mind. The word *business*, by its having no plural number, intimates a particular employ. By the singular of *affairs* being seldom in use in the sense before us, that word is understood to mean a variety of transactions."

The New Standard Dictionary (1936) states that "business" is "any occupation connected with the operations or details of trade or industry" and "is ordinarily for profit, while occupation may be a matter of learning, philanthropy, or religion," and shows very clearly, in contrast, just how the word has been specialized under the impact of a century's change in industrial techniques.

28. A letter from a distinguished attorney inquires, "Wouldn't all this constitutional bother have been avoided, if the grant of power had been in terms of a broad concept, such as business or industry, and not a narrow one such as commerce?"

29. Bernard Mandeville, *The Fable of the Bees, or, Private Vices, Publick Benefits,* 1713. The definition is given as a gloss on his stanza:

> "All Arts and Crafts neglected lie;
> Content, the Bane of Industry,
> Makes 'em admire their homely store,
> And neither seek nor covet more."

30. Thomas R. Malthus, *Definitions in Political Economy,* 1827. It is interesting to note that Malthus bemoans the fact that terms of political economy "which had been settled long ago . . . with a great approach toward correctness by Adam Smith have of late been called in question and altered."

31. In the economic literature of the period there are many comparisons between "the industry of the towns" and agriculture "as the industry of the country."

32. The adjective "industrious" still retains the flavor of ancient usage; the noun eventually left home. In time it came to be the word for an aggregation of enterprises turning out a particular commodity. Almost with the present century it became the popular abstraction for the prevailing economic order. Such expressions as "the coal industry," "the industrial system," and the National Industrial Recovery Act would have been wholly unintelligible in 1787.

33. Kersey, Perry, Martin.

34. Adam Smith remarks, "No large country, it must be observed, ever did or could subsist without some sort of manufactures being carried on in it; and when it is said of any such country that it has no manufactures, it must always be understood of the finer or more improved sort, or as such as are fit for distant sale. In every large country, both the clothing and household furniture of the far greater part of the people are the produce of their own industry. This is even more universally the case in those poor countries which are commonly said to have no manufactures than in those rich ones that are said to abound in them." *Wealth of Nations* (Cannan ed.), I, p. 378.

35. In all the dictionaries examined these words appear as synonyms. In fact in most of the smaller dictionaries of the period each of the three is defined in terms of the other two.

36. Kenrick, Ash. *Oxford English Dictionary*.

37. Farrand, II, pp. 370, 373.

38. *Oxford English Dictionary. Act* 43 *Eliz.* c.2. (1601) entitled, "An Act for setting to work all such persons . . . [who] use no ordinarie or dialie trade of lief to get their living by" shows this usage, which was still common until the middle of the Eighteenth Century. Kersey (1721), and Defoe, B. N., *A Compleat English Dictionary* (1737) both define it thus in their dictionaries, but this meaning is not given by a lexicographer after 1755. The *Oxford English Dictionary* reports that it is completely obsolete today except in Scotland where, in certain sections, "tred" continues in some rural districts to mean *tread, trade,* and *occupation*.

39. Coke, R., *Discourse on Trade*, 1670, p. 1.

40. "The Liberal Arts and Sciences are such as are Noble and Genteel, viz., Grammar, Rhetorick, Musick, Physick, Mathematicks &c." Bailey.

41. Johnson, Rider, Dyche, Barclay, Kenrick, Ash, Entick, Scott, Marchant.

42. For the development of the word see *Oxford English Dictionary*. "Commerce" has been used in English only since the Sixteenth Century, at which time it began to supplant the older term "merchandise."

43. Martin's definition is typical: "*Commerce* (of *commercium*, lat., of *con*, together, and *mercor*, to buy). 1. Traffick, dealing, merchan-

dise, buying and selling, bartering of wares"; *cf.* Johnson, "exchange of one thing for another, interchange of anything; trade, traffick"; Marchant, "exchange of one thing for another; barter, trade, traffic, the buying and selling of all manner of commodities, in order to gain by the same."

44. The synonyms given for "commerce" in this sense are amazingly varied. See Kersey, "Intercourse of Society, Converse or Correspondence"; Martin, "Intercourse, Society, Correspondence, Acquaintance"; Dyche, "conversation by word or letter; correspondence of any kind." *Cf.* Johnson, Kenrick, Rider, Barclay.

It is obvious that when Chief Justice Marshall asserted that "Commerce," as written in the Constitution, "undoubtedly is traffic, but it is something more—it is intercourse" (*Gibbons v. Ogden,* 9 Wheat. 1), he was not giving an abstract concept a push in the direction his judgment convinced him was desirable. He was merely stating a usage that had been set down in the lexicons for over a century.

45. This distinction is not found in the first edition of 1755, but is added in the sixth edition of 1785, the last that the learned Doctor himself revised before his death. Since the distinction is given under the heading "commerce," it would seem that that word in Johnson's mind was, historically, the term used to denote both domestic and international dealings with wares, but that promiscuous usage had wiped out the difference and made all three equivalent.

46. Barclay's dictionary was published in 1782, three years before the sixth edition of Johnson. From Barclay's main definition of *commerce* as "the exchange of commodities, or the buying and selling of merchandize, both at home and abroad, in order to gain profit, and increase the conveniences of life," it is obvious that in his mind "commerce" was adequate to denote both domestic and international dealings. His statement that: "*trade* and *commerce*" relates "to buying and selling; with this difference, that *trade* seems to imply the manufacturing and vending of merchandize within ourselves; *commerce,* negociating with other countries," can only be intended to set off "trade" from the greater and more magnificent word "commerce."

47. The title of the massive opus of that voluminous writer, Malachy Postlethwayt, Esq., entitled, *The Universal Dictionary of Trade and Commerce,* 1766, *may* show either an example of the difference between "trade" and "commerce" mentioned by Johnson and Barclay or the author's desire for a high-sounding title. At any rate, the author uses the terms in the body of the book indiscriminately. In

the main, the work is a discussion of the trade laws, products, and internal police of Europe, Asia, and the American plantations. But the author pauses long enough to puff the grandeur of commerce and trade. He declares: *"Commerce* being the subject of this work, it may be necessary to say something on this head; not by way of declamation which is as needless as haranguing learnedly on the benefit of the air, rain, and sunshine, when nature requires them; but in order to show, that the province of the trader is not so contemptible a class in the community, as some would affect to make it."

"So far is Trade from being inconsistent with the character of a Gentleman in England it makes Gentlemen and hath peopled this nation with Nobles and Gentlemen."

Postlethwayt then lists some of the "Statesmen, Parliamentmen, Privy Councillors, Judges, Bishops, and Noblemen" who have been "in commerce" and who have raised the "splendor and power" of Great Britain by establishing manufactures.

48. It is interesting to note how universal was the idiom "in commerce." A trio of dictionaries sets off "a bank of earth" from a "repository of money" or a "bank, in commerce." "Exchange" is the "giving or receiving one thing for another" but "in commerce, it is the fixing of the actual value of money between different countries." And in like manner "company"—which is ordinarily "an assembly or number of people met together in the same place"—denotes "in commerce, a society of merchants, traders or mechanics joined together in one common interest." Rider, Barclay, Marchant.

49. The ethical implications of words are of the utmost importance. As moral notions change, and an object of taboo comes to be tolerated and later accepted, it must usually come to respectability with a changed name. The classic example is the acceptance by Christian nations—and the reception into Christian doctrine—of usury, rechristened interest. Usury is by far the better word as expressing payment for the *use* of money, but its moral stigma was too flagrant to be erased. Thus it remains as the charge not to be allowed, the sum in excess of the legal rate of interest.

50. It even covered the trade of fishing for "Fisheries denote the Commerce of Fish, more especially the catching them for Sale." Binnell, *Description of the Thames,* 1758, p. 256.

51. Blake, William, *King Edward the Third,* c. 1775.

52. Goldsmith's *Traveller*, 1765.

53. A rather cursory examination of poetical allusions to "commerce" shows a decided division of opinion as to its effects. Cowper in *The Sofa*, 1783, l. 719, applauds and asks:

"Where has commerce such a mart
So rich, so thronged, so drained, and so supplied,
As London, opulent, enlarged, and still
Increasing London?"

David Humphrey, an American, in *A Poem on Industry*, 1794, l. 12, also expresses approbation and hope that

". . . soon shall Commerce, better understood,
Teach happier barter for the mutual good."

But Shelley in his *Queen Mab*, 1813, is downright bitter; the industrial revolution had begun to show in his time its most ugly features, and so it is:

"Commerce! beneath whose poison-breathing shade
No solitary virtue dares to spring;
But poverty and wealth, with equal hand,
Scatter their withering curses."

54. As yet American usage was English usage. A native vernacular was in the making, and there was already the beginning of an American language. But the patriots who sat at Philadelphia had all been born English citizens; and in the realm of government and politics —where intercourse in ideas and wares was habitual—the two vocabularies were still almost identical. See H. L. Mencken, *The American Language*, 1936.

It was not until 1828 that Noah Webster produced the first *American Dictionary of the English Language*. In his pages these eighteenth-century meanings of the words of trade linger on as yet little touched by a changing American usage.

CHAPTER IV

1. Edmund Burke, John Charles Fox, and Adam Smith are but the most conspicuous of the large group in England that "sympathized" with American aspirations.

2. Mun, Thomas, *England's Treasure by Forraign Trade, Or, The*

Balance of Our Forraign Trade is the Rule of Our Treasure, 1664. Mun has been called "the founder of the mercantile system," and Adam Smith states that his title was held as the fundamental maxim in political economy not only of England but of all other commercial countries. However, the roots of mercantilism as a national policy reach back to much earlier times and even the balance of trade doctrine was tentatively set forth as early as the Fourteenth Century. See Horrocks, J. W., *A Short History of Mercantilism,* 1925, pp. 30-85.

3. It is usually overlooked that the "common" were set in contra-distinction to the private callings. They were not like the public utilities of today, a few trades which, because of a peculiar relation to the public, were singled out for separate treatment. Instead they included all the callings which came to market and were for hire.

4. It is of interest that in the textile revolution—a mere aspect of the industrial revolution—the new inventions originated in the cotton manufactures. The woolen trade was of such importance to the state that it had been minutely controlled; the cotton trade, of little consequence, had been left unregulated.

5. See *Encyclopedia of the Social Sciences,* Individualism.

6. A qualification must be set down here, for Franklin at least as early as 1774 repeats the anecdote lifted from the Physiocrats that gave the phrase to the world. Perhaps, in general, he says, "it would be better if government meddled no farther with trade, than to protect it, and let it take its course. Most of the statutes . . . for regulating, directing, or restraining trade, have, we think, been either political blunders, or jobs obtained by artful men for private advantage, under pretense of public good. When Colbert assembled some wise old merchants . . . and desired their advice . . . how he could best serve and promote commerce, their answer . . . was in three words only, *Laissez-nous faire:* 'Let us alone.' It is said by a very solid writer of the same nation . . . *Pas trop gouverner:* 'Not to govern too much.' Which, perhaps, would be of more use when applied to trade, than in any other public concern."

However, notice, as in the case of Adam Smith, this is an attack on the grounds of expediency; a plea for regulation that does not lay itself open to exploitation by "artful men"; that does not truly add to the wealth of the nation.

7. Adam Smith is only the most conspicuous. As Harold J. Laski

notes in the *Rise of Liberalism*, 1936, Chap. II, there had been individuals pointing in the direction of *laissez-faire* for a hundred years previously, and arguing as did Smith against the inexpediency of specific acts.

8. Burney, Charles, *A General History of Music*. This work, which puts the art in its social and ideological setting, occasionally reveals a peculiarity of its age in an appeal to the "natural harmonies." The first volume appeared in 1776.

9. The Eighteenth Century was restrained, but realistic. It was the Nineteenth Century, with its system-building which, under the joint intellectual influence of theology and of physics, converted the state into an abstraction. The antithesis of group and state likewise became dominant in opinion somewhat later.

10. The choice of a word is often an indulgence in other matters. It was something of an affectation for the thirteen colonies, after Independence, to call themselves States; for it is difficult to set up criteria by which all of them could qualify. But their state of mind and the poverty of language conspired to make them States. And national events had to take the consequences.

11. In the Eighteenth Century, with the state as the dominant agent of regulation, the relation of economics and politics was very close. "Economics" was the science, rules or art of managing "the affairs of a family, state or community" after "a commodious and regular manner grounded upon experience and a regular chain of consequences following from certain premises laid down." (Dyche, Marchant.) Hence "political economy."

12. The quotation is from Turgot's *Eloge de Gourney*. Quoted in Laski's, *The Rise of Liberalism*, p. 208.

13. Anderson, p. XVI. The author states that he has written the book because "a *Chronological and General History of Commerce* is, to this day, quite an untrodden path as comprehending therein the discoveries, inventions and improvements in navigation, colonization, manufactures, agriculture, and their relative arts and branches," p. VIII.

14. Smith, Adam, *Lectures on Justice, Police, Revenue, and Arms* (Cannan ed.), p. 160.

15. Smith, *Wealth of Nations*, I, p. 356.

16. *Ibid.*, I, p. 24.

17. This is the first sentence of the *Wealth of Nations*. The phrase "necessities and conveniences"—or variants of it—appears again and again in the economic vocabulary of the time. Locke, before 1700, states that "the intrinsic worth of anything consists in its fitness to supply the necessities or serve the conveniences of human life." (*Essay on Money*, etc., ed. 1696, p. 7.) Tench Coxe, American political economist, uses the phrase (*View of the United States*, p. 24). And the aged Madison, man of the Eighteenth Century, drawing up in 1832 a preface for the *Debates in the Convention*, sets down that "Weakness and the wants of man" naturally lead to an association of individuals into society for safety, the advantages of social intercourse, and "the exchange of the necessaries and comforts of life." Farrand, III, p. 539.

18. Smith, *Wealth of Nations*, I, p. 356.

19. This explains the dictionary definitions of both Barclay and Rider that "commerce" is "the exchange of commodities . . . at home and abroad, in order to gain profit and increase the conveniences of life." It explains Barclay's statement, obvious to his contemporaries, that "trade and commerce" relate to "buying and selling" and imply the "manufacture and vending" of "merchandize." It explains, too, the rather hopeless feeling Dyche shows when he tries to define "exchange" in a few words, as "giving one thing for another, *which really and indeed includes* all merchandize, traffick, bargains, and sales, *whatever*."

20. Smith, *Wealth of Nations*, I, p. 355. Smith, it will be remembered, did not believe with the Physiocrats that "the gain of the town is the loss of the country."

21. Production was a grand rationalization of an interest. The verb "to produce" meant "to bring forth, to cause, to generate," and the kindred adjective meant "fertile, generative, efficient." "Production" was presently "the act of producing," a "bringing forth or lengthening," a "fruit or product," "a composition, a work, a publication." Barclay, Ash.

The word did not savor of book and candle. It had not yet been seized upon by the economists, subjected to their tricks of abstraction, and been set down—along with exchange, distribution, and consumption—as four great provinces of the science of wealth. In fact for many years after 1787 so academic a use of the concept was impossible.

22. The way in which the mind can move from one climate of opinion to another is neatly illustrated in a sentence from Carl Becker's *The Heavenly City of the Eighteenth Century Philosophers:* "Newton was as firmly persuaded as any saint that the heavens declare the glories of God; but he was curious to discover, by looking through a telescope and doing a sum in mathematics, exactly how they contrived it."

23. The God in the Declaration of Independence is Nature's God—that is a deistic God. In Mr. Jefferson's first draft God is spelled with a little "g."

24. This was due perhaps to the fact that from 1688 until the Reform Bill of 1832, the squirearchy was so strongly entrenched in Parliament that rationalization was not needed to buttress actual power and privilege.

25. As usual the scholars have all but overlooked the common-sense beliefs—which were far the more important and of which the speculative system was but a philosophical refinement. The popular ideas were just as popular in England as in France. But in France the repressive measures of Colbert designed to foster the industry of the towns gave rise to a unified complaint from the agricultural classes, less privileged than in England, that eventually became refined into the doctrinaire proposals of the Physiocrats. As Laski points out, the Physiocrats by their criticisms of mercantile practices provided an arsenal for the yet-to-be-born propounders of *laissez-faire*, despite the fact that the French thinkers looked to the authority and regulation of a benevolent despot to achieve *their* fostering of agriculture and the wealth of nations.

It is obvious that the dogma of the Physiocrats was a two-edged sword. The notion that the land alone is productive was easily transformed to the proposition that agriculture alone was a beneficial activity for man. But the "laws of Nature" as an ideological prop yield dubious support; for Nature becomes the hero, and Art the villain, in the piece, and it is difficult to hold that legislative policy—even for the promotion of agriculture—is not a work of art and of man.

26. "Policy," says Rider, is "the art of government as it respects foreign powers," while "polity is the art of governing and well-regulating states." Note the phrase "internal polity" in the Declaration of Rights of the first Congress issued in 1774. At that date the colonists, though not yet ready for independence, were contending

that "taxation and internal polity" should be regulated only by a legislature in which they were represented.

27. These terms, indigenous to the Eighteenth Century, appear in several distinct forms, and have finally come to rest as the public safety, public health, public morals, and public welfare of a people.

28. "The police power" of today occupies but a fragment of the province of "the police" of old.

29. It cannot be stressed too much that the national "policy or polity" was still the "system of laws, orders, and regulations of a state." This "combination of many things operating together," this scheme of state in which "the several parts are bound together, follow, or depend on each other" differed little in its essential form from the system of the Middle Ages "instituted of God." The eighteenth-century thinkers were skeptical of the apologies of the clergy, but they did not doubt that "principles of Nature" were eternal and fundamental. Newton had discovered the laws of the physical world in the Seventeenth Century; the men of the following century set out to discover the laws that ruled the social world.

The very word "regulate" with its implication of "adjust" and "set in order" carried with it the idea that authority must discover and channel the actions of the individual that the eternal laws might be allowed to operate to the best advantage.

30. A duty—even though a custom duty—could be made to serve two masters. To the extent that it yielded revenue it seduced policy from its nationalistic purpose of excluding the commodities of the foreigner.

31. Bernard Mandeville's *Fable of the Bees or Private Vices, Publick Benefits.*

32. The spirit of nationalism goes back to the Tudors. The Elizabethan plays, especially Shakespeare, are full of allusions to the worth, the repute, and the prestige of England.

33. Horrocks, *A Short History of Mercantilism,* gives a general view of the system as it prevailed in Europe. It devotes attention to its origins and to the features which have survived. For British mercantilism, see William Cunningham's *Industry and Commerce,* esp. I, pp. 467-72, 481-3, and II, pp. 13-24. The studies of G. L. Beer place their emphasis on the expression of mercantilism in colonial policy, but are indispensable for a study of the system as it evolved.

34. Furniss, E. S., *The Position of the Laborer in the System of Nationalism; A Study in the Labor Theories of the Later English Mercantilists*, 1920, complements the last volume of Beer with a brilliant study of the internal system of regulation upon which the international competition for markets was grounded.

35. Rider.

36. Note the striking contrast between the heinous offense of the bankrupt, who could be punished severely for his crime, and the easy indulgence allowed to the landed gentry in respect to the debts which they owed to tradesmen.

37. Martin, Kersey, Rider.

38. Young, Arthur, *Eastern Tour*, 1771, IV, p. 361, quoted in Furniss, p. 120.

39. Furniss, pp. 117-198, devotes two carefully documented chapters to a discussion of the eighteenth-century concept of wages and the utility of poverty. A typical expression of the period is found in a quotation from *Thoughts on the Present State of the Poor*, published in 1776, by an anonymous author, that "it is observable that where the highest wages are given there they do the least work; and in places where men can earn half a crown . . . a day, they seldom work above three or four days in the week, spend the rest of their money at the alehouse and leave their families to starve at home." (Quoted p. 123.) Furniss concludes that: "So many and positive are the statements of this effect of high wages that we are compelled to admit their truth and to conclude that the labor supply . . . decreased as wages rose." (p. 118.)

40. An obvious fact that exponents of lower wages had to face was that a great decrease in the laborer's purchasing power would injure the landed interest by diminishing the demand for foodstuffs. In fact the money wages of the period as a result of the Justice's assessments were comparatively stable and unchanging. But lower *real wages*, attained by increased prices of food, proved practical and appealed to the land-owning interest. The Corn Laws, passed in 1770 and kept on the statute books for the next half century, were early defended on this ground. The excise on articles of food, too, was relied on by some of its proponents to raise prices to the consumer and thus increase the industry of the people.

41. William Temple's *Essay on Trade and Commerce*, 1770, gives an interesting example of their way of thought. "That idleness is

the consequence of cheap living may be gathered from a knowledge of human nature alone. Mankind . . . are naturally so fond of ease and indolence that they will not labor while they have the means of idleness in their power; but, as soon as these means are exhausted, necessity again arouses them to their work; and from this cause no state has ever yet made any considerable figure in commerce, where the necessaries of life could be obtained by little labor."

42. Heckscher, Eli F., *The Continental System*, 1922, p. 28.

43. Beer, George Louis, *The Origins of the British Colonial System*, 1908, p. 156.

44. Even the parson of the Church of England, with never a prick of conscience, had his wines and brandies regularly from the smuggler. *Woodforde, The Diary of a Country Parson*, 1935 ed. For a historically correct account of the smuggler and his ways see Rudyard Kipling's *A Smuggler's Song* in *Puck of Pook's Hill*.

45. Heckscher, pp. 16-17.

46. *Ibid.*, p. 187 ff.

47. Beer, *British Colonial Policy, 1754-1765*, 1907, p. 133.

48. When the crusade of James I against tobacco was at its height, the Virginia colonists, in response to royal wish, agreed of their free will to reduce acreage, but refused to be bound by contract. They insisted that "many and unspeakable are the miseryes of a contract." Beer, *Origins*, p. 156.

49. An anonymous author on the *State of the Silk and Woolen Trades*, 1713, at p. 3, states: "'Tis a truth generally recognized that as the wealth and riches of the nation consist in trade, so is that trade of more or less worth to that nation by the manufactures that are in it, especially when to make these manufactures little or no materials which compose them are imported from abroad but are the product of our country, as in the case of our woolen manufacture. But this advantage would be of but little profit if those manufactures were not exported into foreign parts, there exchanged for money or for materials absolutely necessary . . . to prevent the exportation of our coin into other countries."

50. Philip Cantillon, in *The Analysis of Trade, Commerce, Coin, Bullion, Banks, and Foreign Exchanges*, 1759, set out "to convey a general Idea of Trade, and its Influence upon and Consequence to Society . . . wishing most sincerely that what I say may raise in

Gentlemen of Power and Influence, a Spirit to take this matter into their serious Considerations; and by reforming the Abuses crept into the Commerce of this Country, to prevent . . . inexpressible misfortune which must attend Posterity by the Loss of Trade. . . ."

51. Cantillon, of course, as the typical uncompromising mercantilist, emphasizes "the Birth of foreign Trade" which, springing from the dissatisfaction of the individual with "bare Provision for the Necessaries of Life," supplies the "Wants of one country with the Superfluities of another." "This Species of Commerce" is "the high Road of Riches and Preferment" and "foreign Commerce and Force of Arms" are the "Two Methods in Nature by which Nations become Powerful and Great." *Ibid.*, p. V.

Adam Smith attaches the greater importance to the internal trade of a nation. "The great commerce of every civilized society is that carried on between the inhabitants of the town and those of the country. It consists in the exchange of crude for manufactured produce, either immediately, or by the intervention of money. . . . The country supplies the town with the means of subsistence, and the materials of manufacture. The town repays this supply by sending back a part of the manufactured produce . . ." *Wealth of Nations*, I, p. 355.

The distinguished Scottish philosopher is a pioneer in the things he has to say about mercantilism; but his use of terms—in particular commerce—is in accord with the usage of his day.

52. Compare the trim dialectical lines of the stereotyped refutation of mercantilist fallacies in a book on the *Principles of Economics* with the hard realism of Adam Smith's unsympathetic attack on mercantilistic practices.

53. Compare Laski, Chap. III. Here, as elsewhere, there is danger that sentences lifted from their context will be endowed with the ideas of another age.

54. A study should be made of citations from the *Wealth of Nations* in the United States Reports. No layman is so often cited as Adam Smith; and yet usually the economic philosophy of a later individualism is read into his eighteenth-century lines.

55. *Wealth of Nations*, Vol. I, p. 395. Compare Franklin's statement that there seems to be "but three ways for a nation to acquire wealth. The first is by *war*, as the Romans did, in plundering their conquered neighbors. This is *robbery*. The second by *commerce*,

which is generally *cheating*. The third by *agriculture*, the only honest way, wherein man receives a real increase of the seed thrown into the ground, in a kind of continual miracle, wrought by the hand of God in his favor." *Works*, II, p. 376.

56. Here is a step along the way of abstraction. A landed interest appears as land, a commercial interest as capital. A later addition of labor—as yet quite inarticulate—completes the trio of factors of production. Later a more personalized entrepreneur is added. In the likeness of these abstract factors appear abstract distributive shares—rent, interest, wages and profits. With the change the older questions are lost, issues of public policy between interest reappear as the principle of an automatic economic order, and political economy passes on into economics. The subject obtrudes into the Constitution of 1787 as political economy; it appears in recent judicial utterances as economics.

57. Aside from Magna Carta, the Constitution, and certain passages in the Bible, it is hard to think of any document so distorted by an *ex post facto* gloss as the *Wealth of Nations*.

It is an enlightening commentary on the uses of posterity that Smith's violent denunciation and attack on the most powerful vested interests and special privileges of his day should be the stout dialectical bulwark for the same type of interests in 1937.

58. It is noteworthy that the first measure considered by the First Congress under the Constitution after its procedural rules were established was a tariff. It was not only designed to produce revenue but also to be "adequate" in its operation to the situation of the Union as it "respects our agriculture, our manufactures, and our commerce." *Annals of Congress*, 1834; H. R. vol. I, p. 102, 1st Cong. 1st Session.

59. As William Graham Sumner points out in his *Life of Alexander Hamilton*, 1896, p. 31, the revolt of the colonies was a reaction of the mercantile system against itself. When the actual break with England came the colonists counted heavily upon the intervention of France, Spain, or Holland as their allies. This hope was in part predicated on the knowledge that any of the great powers would be glad to weaken England's competing position by severing her colonies. But the rebels relied for support mainly on the offer of trade with an area that had been England's prized "sole market." England had said that the colonial trade was an invaluable possession. The French,

on the grounds of eighteenth-century political economy, believed it, and it was French aid that led to Yorktown.

60. Letter to Joseph Reed, December 12, 1778, *Works* (Ford ed.), VII, p. 288.

61. A later age, intent upon its own ways of thought, has made Adam Smith the Father of Political Economy. The doctrines of the Nineteenth Century stem from his writings, but they create an economy from which politics has been almost eliminated. Political economy is, of course, much older; and the coming of *laissez-faire* marks its passage into economics.

62. "You ask what I think on the expediency of encouraging our States to be commercial? Were I to indulge my own theory, I should wish them to practice neither commerce nor navigation, but to stand, with respect to Europe, precisely on the footing of China. We should thus avoid wars, and all our citizens would be husbandmen. Whenever, indeed, our numbers should so increase as that our produce would overstock the markets of those nations who should come to seek it, the farmers must either employ the surplus of their time in manufactures, or the surplus of our hands must be employed in manufactures, or in navigation. But that day would, I think, be distant, and we should long keep our workmen in Europe, while Europe should be drawing rough materials and even subsistence from America."—To Count van Hogendorp, 1785, IV, p. 104.

63. Franklin, *Works*, IV, p. 19.

64. Jefferson, however, after his experience in the Presidency, changed his views on the value of manufactures to the nation. The wars in Europe and "a profligacy of power to exclude us from the field of intercourse with foreign nations" had created a necessity of domestic manufactures. "We must place the manufacturer by the side of the agriculturist. . . . Shall we make our own comforts or go without them at the will of a foreign nation? He, therefore, who is now against domestic manufacture, must be for reducing us either to dependence on that foreign nation, or to be clothed in skins, and to live, like wild beasts, in dens and caverns. I am not one of these; experience has taught me that manufactures are now as necessary to our independence as to our comfort."—To Benjamin Austin, January, 1816; X, p. 8.

65. In the America of after-the-Revolution the belief in the balance of trade then was prevalent, and specific taxes were attacked or

defended in its terms. See the arguments in favor of the duty on imports—which the Confederation never passed—drawn up by Madison, Ellsworth, and Hamilton. They argued that the tax was passed on to the consumer: "Every class of the community bears its share of the duty in proportion to its consumption, which last is regulated by the comparative wealth of the respective classes, in conjunction with their habits of expense or frugality. The rich and luxurious pay in proportion to their riches and luxury; the poor and parsimonious in proportion to their poverty and parsimony. A chief excellence of this mode of revenue is, that it preserves a just measure to the abilities of individuals, promotes frugality, and taxes extravagance." Elliot, I, p. 100.

66. It must, however, be remembered that a criticism of particular practices, such as royal monopolies and trade regulation, helps to prepare the way for *laissez-faire*. It promotes a public opinion favorable to a do-nothing policy, and it supplies concrete instances which, at the touch of speculative thought, may become abstractions.

67. The cry of the harassed commercial men during the crisis of 1787 is against the wasteful luxury of the people. Tench Coxe bemoans the "wanton" consumption, the extravagant and wasteful use of foreign manufactures "that has seen $60,000 in one year" spent for the "finer kind of buttons, buckles, breast-pins" and like "trinkets." He is glad to note that it is in the towns that this "madness for foreign finery rages and destroys," and suggests sumptuary laws to check the "malignant and alarming symptoms, threatening convulsions and dissolution to the political body." *View of the United States*, p. 31.

68. As Sumner points out, this shows how completely they were wedded to the maxims of mercantilism; for to refuse to pay taxes without representation on the grounds of tyranny and to allow regulation of trade, which was far more liable to abuse, was not the strictest of logic.

CHAPTER V

1. Yates' diary, which only covers the debates until the first of July, is included in Farrand. Lansing's journal, covering the same dates, has recently been discovered; it has not yet been published.

2. To some extent the changes in Madison's politics can be followed in the successive editings of the Journal. Luckily for the

scholar the ink used in the emendations has faded differently from that of the original notes set down immediately after each day's deliberations. Emendations in most cases are as distinguishable as if written in red ink.

3. There are notes of speeches delivered by Paterson, Pinckney, Hamilton, Pierce, and others. McHenry also kept journals. The most important of these miscellaneous remains can be found in Farrand.

4. Gustav Schmoller, *The Mercantile System and its Historical Significance*, 1896, p. 57.

5. Debates of August 9th and 13th. Unless otherwise indicated, quotations from the Debates will be from Madison's Journal.

6. This was Gouverneur Morris of Pennsylvania. There is no record that Robert Morris, delegate from the same State, spoke in debate on the floor.

7. The thrust was doubtless aimed at a fellow delegate from his own State, a certain Dr. Benjamin Franklin. Morris on August 23rd had a chance to exhibit his "wholesome prejudices" in favor of America. Laying down a principle for guidance in negotiating treaties, "he wished none to be made with G. Britain till she should be at war. Then a good bargain might be made with her. So with other foreign powers."

8. Wilson himself was foreign-born, as were Hamilton, Robert Morris, Davie, Paterson, Butler, Fitzsimmons, and McHenry.

9. June 25th.

10. The context makes his meaning specific. A national commercial policy was a necessity. Until an urban population of poor laborers made possible firmly established manufactures, the Union would be drained of its specie unless national legislation countered with a positive policy. A scarcity of money bore heavily upon planters who broadened agriculture to include operations in slaves and western lands.

11. Yates reports this "Commerce can never interfere with the government, nor give a complexion to its councils."

12. June 7th. Gerry states that "the people have two great interests, the landed interest, and the commercial including the stockholders [holders of the government debt]. To draw both branches from the people will leave no security to the latter interest; the

people being chiefly composed of the landed interest, and errone-
ously, supposing that the other interests are adverse to it."

13. June 18th.

14. June 6th.

15. Merchant and manufacturer were not mutually exclusive terms.
In 1787 the merchant was often the capitalist who financed the manu-
factory. This coincidence in post-Revolutionary America can be
seen in the petition of "the Merchants, Tradesmen, etc." of Providence, R. I., to the Constitutional Convention, declaring "that full
power for the Regulation of the Commerce of the United States,
both Foreign and Domestic, ought to be vested in the National
Council." One of the signers, John Brown, was a member of the
famous commercial family that financed Samuel Slater, who is hailed
as "the Father of the Cotton Manufacture of America." Farrand,
III, p. 18.

The greatest part of the capital invested in early American manufacturing came from merchants. Especially rapid was the transfer
of capital from foreign commerce during the period 1808-1815 when
the embargo and War of 1812 made domestic investment desirable.

16. June 26th.

17. Madison continues, "It was true as had been observed we had
not among us those hereditary distinctions of rank . . . nor those
extremes of wealth or poverty which characterize the modern states
of Europe. We cannot however be regarded even at this time as one
homogeneous mass. . . . In framing a system which we wish to last
for ages, we should not lose sight of the changes which ages will
produce. An increase of population will of necessity increase the
proportion of those who will labour under all the hardships of life
and secretly sigh for a more equal distribution of its blessings. These
may in time outnumber those who are placed above the feelings of
indigence. According to the equal laws of suffrage, the power will
slide into the hands of the former."

It is interesting to note that Yates, well grounded in the political
economy of the day, translates Madison's "have not's" into the
laboring poor of the commercial cities and translates the "class
struggle" into the facile clash of *agriculture* v. *commerce*. He reports that Madison said:

"Such are the various pursuits of this life, that in all civilized
countries, the interest of a community will be divided. There will

be debtors and creditors, and an unequal possession of property, and hence arises different views and different objects in government . . . The man who is possessed of wealth, who lolls on his sofa or rolls in his carriage, cannot judge of the wants or feelings of the day laborer. The government we mean to erect is intended to last for ages. The landed interest, at present, is prevalent; but in the process of time, when we approximate to the states and kingdoms of Europe, when the number of land holders shall be comparatively small, through the various means of trade and manufactures, will not the landed interest be overbalanced in future elections, and unless wisely provided against, what will become of your government?"

18. July 14th.

19. Gorham's observation on the clause denying election to those "having unsettled accounts" is interesting. Speaking immediately after Madison, he said, "It would put the commercial and manu-facturing part of the people on a worse footing . . ."

20. Hamilton could understand how the North and South as geo-graphical units could have different *"theories"* of commerce, but if they were to be one nation the national good demanded mercantile policies. See Farrand, I, p. 305; notes among Hamilton papers used in delivering his great speech of June 18th.

21. The *Federalist*, X, offers the most lucid and profound insight into the Framers' theory of state. Considering it axiomatic that man is governed by "self-love" and is a "slave of his passions," it follows that each will try to aggrandize himself at the expense of others. The "most frivolous and fanciful" distinctions are enough to set him at his neighbor's throat. However, "the most common and durable source of factions has been the various and unequal distribution of property. Those who hold and those who are without property have ever formed distinct interests in society. Those who are credi-tors and those who are debtors fall under a like discrimination. A landed interest, a manufacturing interest, a mercantile interest, a moneyed interest, with many lesser interests, grow up of necessity in civilized nations, and divide them into different classes, actuated by different sentiments and views. The regulation of these various and interfering interests forms the principal task of modern legisla-tion . . ."

22. August 20th.

23. This vote of August 20th is an interesting commentary on the

"liberty" and fear of the Federal "tyranny" that the Maryland and Delaware delegates had professed during the long hot debates of June.

Mason did not let this initial defeat deter him from a further advocacy of sumptuary regulations on September 13th. "After descanting on the extravagance of our manners, the excessive consumption of foreign superfluities, and the necessity of restricting it, as well with oeconomical as republican views, he moved that a committee be appointed to report articles of association for encouraging by the advice the influence and the example of the Members of the Convention, oeconomy, frugality, and American manufactures."

24. Madison's Journal, May 29th.

25. McHenry's outline is in the following form:

> "3. Incapable to produce certain blessings.
>
> "The benefits of which we are singly incapable cannot be produced by the union. The five per cent impost not agreed; a blessing congress ought to be enabled to obtain.
>
> "Congress ought to posses a power to prevent emissions of bills of credit.
>
> "Under this head may be considered the establishment of great national works—the improvements of inland navigation—agriculture—manufactures—a freer intercourse among the citizens."

26. Debates of August 21st. The thesis that the Fathers understood —and intended—the Federal taxing power to be restricted to purposes of revenue only is contradicted by the whole course of this particular discussion. Brant, Irving, *Storm over the Constitution*, 1936, pp. 164-178 offers a suggestive discussion on this point.

27. August 22nd.

28. August 25th.

29. August 29th.

30. August 29th.

31. It was Madison who stressed this point. *Cf.* the preceding speech of Morris.

32. Ellsworth's remark on August 21. *Cf.* Madison's statement, "If the Wealth of the Eastern States should in still greater proportion

be augmented, that wealth wd. contribute the more to the public wants, and be otherwise a national benefit," on August 29th.

33. August 29th. Mr. Rutledge then went on to mention specifically "the necessity of securing the West India trade," and insisted that "it did not follow from a grant of power to regulate trade, that it would be abused." Madison had already argued that abuse was rendered "improbable" by the two-house legislature, the independence of the Senate and by the Executive veto. Also that the South could always find agrarian allies in Connecticut and New Jersey, the interior districts of even "the most commercial States," and by "the accession of Western States which would be altogether agricultural."

34. August 18th. Forty years later, during the controversy over the tariff, it was argued that failure to include this clause in the Constitution was proof that the Convention did not intend to grant Congress power to foster manufactures by commercial regulations. Madison, after calling attention to the first tariff drawn by a Congress containing sixteen Framers in its membership, insisted that such an inference was ridiculous. The propositions might have been disapproved "because they were in bad form or not in order; because they blended other powers with the particular power in question; or because the object had been, or would be elsewhere provided for." Letter to Professor Davis, dated 1832, given in Farrand, III, p. 520.

35. August 20th.

36. September 14th. A corporation is "a body politic authorized by the King's charter to have a common seal" and "able by their common consent to grant or receive in law anything agreeable to their charter" and "to sue and to be sued even as one man." Rider, Marchant. Note the plural and the consciousness with which the personal analogy is being imposed on the body politic.

Madison had proposed the same power earlier, on August 18th.

37. September 14th.

38. Farrand, II, p. 640. Gerry also has left the reasons for his refusal to sign. Number six reads: "Commercial powers authorize monopolies & companys." (p. 636.)

39. For the contemporary meaning of the word and its implications, *vd., supra*, pp. 79-80.

40. August 29th.

41. September 3rd.

42. "The power of establishing uniform laws of bankruptcy is so intimately connected with the regulation of commerce, and will prevent so many frauds where parties or their property may lie or be removed into different States, that the expediency of it seems not likely to be drawn into question." *Federalist Papers*, XLI.

43. It is, of course, not to be argued that in an attempt to give exactness to the words of the great charter, the delegates sought out meanings in the dictionaries. That would be the way of lawyers concerned with the meticulous statement of reciprocal obligations in a contractual document. It is not the way of men-of-affairs seeking words of broad import with which to establish a Federal Government and endow it with broad powers. Besides the currency of words of such universal usage made no such recourse necessary. The speech of the Fathers, as much as the cut of their clothes, their gracious manner, and their quaint rhetoric, belong to the age in which they lived. In all their foresight the Fathers did not anticipate the distinctive judicial usage of the fourth decade of the Twentieth Century.

44. In a technical sense "trade" is not endowed in any dictionary with such elaborateness of meaning as "intercourse" or "correspondence."

45. A strange twist of the eighteenth-century mind is not without interest. In 1762 a number of citizens of Amherst, Northampton, Hatfield, and Hadley, in Massachusetts, drew up a petition to the King for a royal charter. Among their persuasive arguments was the use of higher learning as a means of military defense. They sought "that Inlargement and Security which our ancestors . . . prayed for, but never saw. . . . The County of Hampshire has been . . . exposed to the Invasion and Depredations of our French and Indian Enemies. . . . Our blood has been poured out like water, and the Bodies of Men, Women, and Children have been given to be meat for the Beasts of the Land!" It was probable that "the School would attract many persons of small Fortunes, Who by worthy motives, would be led to engage in preaching and propagating Christianity among the Indians. . . . Whereby the Redeemer's Kingdom . . . would be promoted and inlarged" and the Six Nations would be "more firmly attached to your Majesty's Government." Long, J. C., *Lord Jeffery Amherst*, pp. 172-173.

46. The Articles of Confederation had ostensibly vested in Congress the "sole and exclusive right and power of . . . regulating the trade and managing all affairs with the Indians." In reality it was another instance of a simulacrum of power, for the States reserved the right to regulate the Indians within their borders and did so with little regard to Congress and the interests of other States. The Committee of Detail evidently intended to write in a clause remedying the situation but inadvertently left it out of the first draft of the Constitution. Madison on August 18th moved to correct the omission by allowing Congress "to regulate the affairs with the Indians, as well within as without the limits of the United States." This was reworded by committee into a more restricted form and reported out August 22nd but not acted upon. Finally on September 4th, without discussion, the phrase "and with the Indian Tribes" was added to the commerce clause.

47. August 16th.

48. See Adam Smith's remark on this aspect of regulation: "Though the encouragement of exportation, and the discouragement of importation, are the two great engines by which the mercantile system proposes to enrich every country, yet it reverses its policy on some commodities. For it *discourages* the exportation of the materials of manufacture, and of the instruments of trade, in order to give our own workmen an advantage . . . and by restraining in this manner, the export of a few commodities, of no great price, it proposes to occasion a much greater and more valuable exportation of others. It encourages the importation of the materials of manufacture in order that our people may be enabled to work them up more cheaply, and thereby prevent a greater and more valuable importation of the manufactured commodities." *Wealth of Nations*, II, p. 141.

49. August 21st.

50. Debate of August 21st.

51. This argument was advanced during the first debate on the prohibition on August 16th.

52. Debate of August 21st.

53. "Mr. Fitzsimmons would be against a tax on exports to be laid immediately; but was for giving a power of laying the tax when a proper time may call for it. This would certainly be the case when America should become a manufacturing Country.—He illustrated his argument by the duties in G. Britain on wool &c."

54. *Vd.*, *infra*, pp. 174-176.

55. Remark made by Sherman on August 16th.

56. Adam Smith leveled this very charge against "the merchants and manufacturers," who had been "by far the principal architects" of the English system. "Consumption is the sole end of all production; and the interest of the producer ought to be attended to only so far as it may be necessary for promoting that of the consumer. But in the mercantile system the interest of the consumer is almost constantly sacrificed to that of the producer; and it seems to consider production, and not consumption as the sole end and object of all industry and commerce." *Wealth of Nations*, II, p. 159.

57. Randolph's First Resolution. It is a variation of a phrase in the Articles of Confederation.

58. The Sixth Resolution of the Virginia plan.

59. Connecticut, however, was divided.

60. The rather unusual word "incompetent" *may* have been lifted by some of the Virginians from Pelatiah Webster's pamphlet of 1783 entitled, *"A Dissertation on the Political Union and Constitution of the Thirteen United States of North America, which is Necessary to their Preservation and Happiness."* His proposal: "The Powers of Congress . . . shall be restricted to such matters of general authority and utility to all the States as cannot come within the jurisdiction of any particular State or to which the authority of any particular State is not *competent.*"

61. July 17th.

62. In full the rewritten clause gave to the National Legislature the power "to legislate in all cases for the general interests of the Union, and also in those to which the States are separately incompetent or in which the harmony of the United States may be interrupted by the exercise of individual Legislation."

63. Randolph also damned it as redundant: "The last member of the sentence is also superfluous being included in the first."

64. The various plans, proposals, and whatnots utilized by the Committee of Detail is to be found in Farrand, II.

65. Under the quota system of the Confederation each State was assessed by the Congress for its share of the revenue necessary to meet fiscal obligations of the Union. The system was unsatisfactory

from the first. State after state wrangled over the amount it was supposed to pay or was indifferent to the demand. Since there was no means of enforcing the revenue requirements, the Government of the Confederation throughout its existence teetered on the verge of bankruptcy.

66. Until recent times famines were of frequent occurrence. The practice of conserving food and other necessities for home consumption through the use of embargoes was common even in the Eighteenth Century.

67. Farrand, II, p. 243. Congress in addition to calling upon states for Quotas was to be "authorized to pass Acts for raising a Revenue, by levying a Duty or Duties on all goods or Merchandizes of foreign growth or manufacture, imported into any part of the United States —by Stamps on Paper Vellum or Parchment—and by a Postage on all Letters and Packages passing through the general Post-Office, to be applied to such federal purposes as they shall deem proper & expedient. . . ."

68. *Ibid.*, II, p. 243.

69. The state courts had original jurisdiction over matters of trade regulation. In numerous instances in suits in commercial law there was delay, indifference, or a lack of mercantile justice. A more competent judiciary was one of the wants of the advocates of a high-toned government.

70. The Paterson plan was a product to which several delegates contributed. In a preliminary draft in Paterson's handwriting the form reads:

Congress (shall be) authorized to pass Acts for the Regulation of Trade as well with foreign Nations as with each other, and for laying such Prohibitions, (in margin: "Imposts Excise—Stamps —Post-Office—Poll Tax") and such Imposts and Duties upon Imports as may be necessary for the purpose. *Ibid.*, III, p. 612.

71. Alexander Hamilton also had submitted a plan on June 18th. Its provision that Congress be empowered "to pass all laws whatsoever" checked only by an absolute veto in the Executive was too strong to be stomached.

72. It was composed of Rutledge of South Carolina, Randolph of Virginia, Wilson of Pennsylvania, Ellsworth of Connecticut, and Gorham of Massachusetts.

73. A document in the handwriting of Randolph with emendation by Rutledge. Each item is checked off showing its use in subsequent drafts. It is given in Farrand, II, p. 137 ff.

74. *Ibid.*, II, pp. 142-143. "agrd 1. To raise money by taxation unlimited as to sum, *for the (future) past (or) & future debts and necessities of the union* and to establish rules for collection." Those words italicized were changes made by Randolph from the original draft. Words in parentheses were crossed out.

75. "Inhabitants" is, of course, a constitutional euphemism for "slaves."

76. At this stage of the proceedings it was expected that navigation acts and all acts for the regulation of trade would require a two-thirds vote of both houses of Congress.

77. *Ibid.*, II, p. 167. "The Legislature of the United States shall have the (Right and) Power to lay and collect Taxes Duties Imposts and Excises; to regulate (Naturalization and) Commerce *with foreign nations & amongst the several States to establish an Uniform Rule for Naturalization etc.*" Section italicized is emendation in Rutledge's handwriting. Words in parentheses were crossed out.

Madison moved on August 18th that Congress have power "to regulate affairs with the Indians as well within as without the U. States." The Committee of Unfinished Parts, accepting the provision but rejecting its form, suggested the simple addition of the five words to the commerce clause. It was agreed to without discussion on September 4th. *Vd., supra.*

78. *Ibid.*, II, p. 308. *Nem. con.* is abbreviated from the Latin *nemine contradicente*, meaning "no one contradicting; unanimously."

79. Randolph's letter on transmitting the Constitution to the Virginia Legislature. It is included in Farrand, III.

80. James Madison to John Tyler, 1833.

81. Note of Major William Pierce on debate of May 31st.

82. June 8th.

83. June 9th (Paterson's notes).

84. June 19th.

85. June 25th.

86. May 31st.

87. James Madison to Richard S. Garnett, February 11, 1824.

88. The call to the Convention "had originated in Virginia," and its delegation felt a peculiar responsibility for the result. They were the first to arrive and in the period of waiting felt they must "be prepared with some materials for the work of the Convention."

On May 20, 1787, George Mason wrote to his son:
"Upon the great principles, . . . I have reason to hope, there will be greater unanimity and less opposition, except from the little States than was at first apprehended. The most prevalent idea in the principal States seems to be a total alteration of the present federal system, and substituting a great national council or parliament consisting of two branches . . . founded upon . . . proportionate representation, with full legislative powers upon all the subjects of the Union. . . ."

89. August 28th. Mason had opposed the government power over exports as tending to reduce the states "to mere corporations" (on August 21st). He and Luther Martin of Maryland seem to have been the most consistent proponents of state sovereignty in the Convention.

It is important to note, however, that this regard for "states rights" was predicated on a desire for regulation by the individual State instead of the National Government. It had no base in *laissez-faire;* it was no denial of the need of regulation.

90. September 15th. It was argued by Madison that the power of Congress to regulate commerce was quite adequate to restrain the states from levying duties for the purpose of "clearing harbors and erecting lighthouses." Sherman confirmed this view. "The power of the United States to regulate trade being supreme can controul interferences of the State regulation when such interferences happen; so that there is no danger to be apprehended from a concurrent jurisdiction."

The Maryland delegation, whose members had "almost shuddered at the fate of the commerce" of their state under the tax power and the commerce clause (McHenry's diary, August 7) had, earlier, been instrumental in writing in the provision that "no preference shall be given by the regulation of commerce or Revenue to the ports of one State. . . ." See debates for August 30th and 31st.

91. September 12th.

92. The clause as rephrased by Mason on September 13th read:

"Provided that no State shall be restrained from imposing the usual duties on produce exported from such State, for the sole purpose of defraying the charges of inspecting, packing, storing, and indemnifying the losses on such produce, while in the custody of public officers; but all such regulations shall in case of abuse, be subject to the revision and controul of Congress."

93. It is significant that Roger Sherman, the reputed expositor of the theory of local government, should have insisted upon removing from the states the power to confuse the regulation of commerce by having the net proceeds of inspection go into the national treasury.

94. As late as 1824 Chief Justice Marshall was setting it down as a truth which did not brook contradiction that "The word among means intermingled with. . . . It may very properly be restricted to that commerce which concerns more states than one. . . . The enumeration presupposes something not enumerated; and that something . . . must be the exclusively internal commerce of a state."—*Gibbons v. Ogden*, 9 Wheat 1.

95. In a footnote it may be set down that it is extravagant to claim for the federal establishment a sole solicitude for commerce; but if a bold spirit should indulge a presumption in favor of the exclusiveness of national authority, there is hardly a shred of available contemporary evidence that can be cited in rebuttal.

96. The converse was, of course, set down by Wilson in the Pennsylvania ratifying convention. "Whatever object of government is confined in its operation and effect within the bounds of a particular State should be considered as belonging to the government of that State." He continues, "But though this principle be sound and satisfactory, its application to particular cases would be accompanied with much difficulty; because in its application room must be allowed for great discretionary latitude of construction of the principle. In order to lessen or remove the difficulty arising . . . on this subject, an enumeration of particular instances, in which the application of the principle ought to take place, has been attempted with much industry and care. . . .

"In forming this system it was proper to give minute attention to the interests of all the parts; but there was a duty of still higher import—to feel and to show a predominating regard to the superior interests of the whole. If this great principle had not prevailed, the plan before us would never have made its appearance. The same principle that was so necessary in forming it is equally necessary in our deliberations whether we should reject or ratify it." Elliot, II, pp. 424, 428.

97. September 12th. Madison fought stoutly for inclusion of this device in the Constitution. He was advocating it in March, 1787, in a letter to Jefferson as a necessary "defensive power" for the national legislature since "however ample the Federal powers may be made, or however clearly their boundaries may be delineated on paper" the States would "easily and continually" manage to "baffle" them. It would not only, he added, preserve the Federal power from encroachment, but also would protect the minorities in the State from "paper money and other unrighteous measures."

Madison included it in the Virginia plan where it was voted acceptance on May 31st. The Committee of Detail's draft did not include it, however, and on August 23rd, being reproposed by Charles Pinckney, it was rejected as awkward and unnecessary. "The laws of the General Government," as Mr. Sherman noted, "being Supreme and paramount." The vote was close; six states to five against the negative.

98. It is clear enough that the Convention meant to accept "judicial review," but it does not follow that their judicial review is the judicial review of today. Note here the injunction imposed upon State Courts to respect Acts of Congress; it seems not to have occurred to the Convention that such an injunction was necessary in respect to the national judiciary.

CHAPTER VI

1. *Letters of George Washington*, Sun Dial ed., p. 211.

2. To William Gordon, July 8, 1783, Ford ed., IX.

3. Washington to the Congress, in Convention, September 17, 1787.

4. To Weedon Butler dated May 2nd, 1788. It is to be found in Farrand, III, p. 303.

5. It need hardly be added that Jefferson contemplated "abuses of power issuing from a very different quarter." Madison continued, "This is a truth of great importance, but not yet sufficiently attended to, and is probably more strongly impressed upon my mind by facts, and reflections suggested by them, than on yours which has contemplated abuses of power issuing from a very different quarter. Wherever there is an interest and a power to do wrong, wrong will gen-

erally be done, and not less readily by a powerful and interested party than by a powerful and interested prince." *Documentary History of the Constitution,* V, p. 88, quoted in Beard's *Economic Interpretation,* p. 159.

6. Hamilton's remark on June 19th. Yates' diary.

7. The four preceding words are in parentheses.

8. Outline of his speech on June 9th explaining the New Jersey plan in Paterson's handwriting. Farrand, I, p. 188.

9. June 16th. Yates' diary.

10. Frightened at the possibility that the "vicious" system of proportional representation would be accepted, certain of the delegates from the small states were crying that it was "improper" to exceed their instructions—that the Convention did not have the power to propose a new type of government.

11. June 20th. Mason later refused to sign the Constitution, because, among other things, "that great power," to regulate commerce, was to be exercised by a mere majority vote of Congress. The requirement of a two-thirds vote in both Houses, he felt, offered the South its only protection against "such rigid and premature regulations . . . as would enable the merchants of the Northern and Eastern States not only to demand an exorbitant freight, but to monopolize the purchase of commodities . . . to the great injury of the landed interest . . ." Elliot, I, p. 495.

12. This statement was made on June 25th. At that date the objective of the small states had become equal representation in the Senate. Compare Wilson's speech on June 30th, when the Convention had become deadlocked. He "lamented that such a disagreement should prevail on the point of representation, as he did not foresee that it would happen on the other point most contested, the boundary between the Genl. & the local authorities." Paterson, in taking notes on this speech, succinctly sets down: "The System of Virginia and the System of Jersey agree as to the Powers," and Yates makes it less specific but as broad: "We all aim at giving the general government more energy."

13. June 29th. Irving Brant, in *Storm over the Constitution,* engagingly develops this thesis. With Hamilton's remark as the keynote he presents a convincing argument that "the great debate" of the Convention cannot be explained in the facile terms of states rights v. nationalism.

14. June 16th.

15. June 8th.

16. June 28th. (Yates' diary.)

17. June 29th.

18. Madison crossed out "they would have different interests from the Atlantic States."

19. June 28th.

20. June 30th. The day before he had stated, "The power of self-defense was essential to the small States. . . . He could never admit that there was no danger of combinations among the large States. They will, like individuals, find out and avail themselves of the advantage to be gained by it."

21. The able Connecticut delegates had offered it as a ground for mutual concession four separate times earlier. Mr. Sherman had proposed it first on June 11th and again on June 20th. During the heated course of debate on June 29th, Dr. Johnson and Ellsworth separately offered it again.

22. June 30th. (Yates' diary.) Madison reports Bedford's threat in slightly different phrases. "The Large States dare not dissolve the confederation. If they do the small ones will find some foreign ally of more honor and good faith, who will take them by the hand and do them justice."

23. These were to include granting exclusive rights to Ports, subjecting American seamen or vessels to duties, regulating the navigation of rivers, and regulating coin. The complete list is to be found in Farrand, III, p. 55.

24. July 16th.

25. Madison to Jared Sparks in 1831. Elliot, I, p. 501.

26. July 5th.

27. July 6th.

28. One must be wary of property; the meaning of the word refuses to abide. In an agrarian economy of self-sufficiency its role is quite different from that played in a commercial economy. As a society passes into commerce, sources of income other than land are opened, property changes its character, and income becomes pe-

cuniary. Hence arise hazards in a carry-over of eighteenth-century
diction.

29. June 30th. (Yates' diary.) *Cf.* Madison's transcription. "Bad Gov-
ernts. are of two sorts. 1. that which does too little. 2. that which
does too much: that which fails thro' weakness; and that which de-
stroys (crossed out 'rules') thro' oppression. Under which of these
evils do the U. States at present groan? Under the weakness and
inefficiency of its Governt. To remedy this weakness we have been
sent to this Convention."

30. For two succinct and scholarly treatments of the political philosophy embodied in the Constitution see Parrington, Vernon L.,
Main Currents in American Thought, I, pp. 279-291, and Beard's *Economic Interpretation*, pp. 152-216. The authors approach the subject
from different angles but arrive at practically identical conclusions.

31. August 14th.

32. *Federalist*, X. This essay of Madison's is perhaps the most enlightening of the series upon the political theories of the Framers
of the Constitution.

33. The Diary of George Washington, 17 September, 1787, quoted
in Farrand, III, p. 81.

34. Richard Henry Lee in *Letters of the Federal Farmer*. It is included in Ford, Paul L., ed., *Pamphlets on the Constitution of the
United States of 1787-1788.*

35. *New Hampshire Spy*, October 27, 1787; *Massachusetts Gazette*,
October 26, 1787. Both of these appeals are quoted in Beard's *Economic Interpretation*, pp. 300-301.

36. *Pennsylvania Gazette*, August 29, 1787. As yet the Constitution
had not been published. The article continues, with colorful description. "The States neglect their roads and canals . . . Trading and
manufacturing companies suspend their voyages and manufactures.
. . . The lawful usurer locks up or buries his specie. . . . The
wealthy farmer views a plantation with desire for one of his sons,
but declines to empty his chest of hard-earned dollars. . . . The
embarrassed farmer and the oppressed tenant, who wish to become
free and independent by emigrating to a frontier country, wait to see
whether they shall be protected by a National force from the Indians
and a National system of taxation from the more terrible pest of
State and county tax gatherers. In short the pulse of industry, in-

genuity, and enterprise in every occupation stand still" until the event is known.

37. Elliot, II, pp. 129-130. Bowdoin earlier had contradicted the criticism that the government being set up had too great a power vested in Congress. "If we consider the objects of the power they are numerous and important; and as human foresight cannot extend to many of them, and all of them are in the womb of futurity, the *quantum* of the power *cannot* be estimated. . . . The respectability of the United States among foreign nations, our commerce with them . . . their estimation of our friendship and fear of losing it, our capacity to resent injuries and our security against interior as well as foreign attacks must be derived from such a power. In short, the commercial and political happiness, the liberty and property, the peace, safety, and general welfare, both internal and external, of each and all the states, depend on that power; which, as it must be applied to a variety of objects, and to cases and exigencies beyond the ken of human prescience, must be very great; and which *cannot* be limited without endangering the public safety." (pp. 84-85.)

38. *Ibid.*, II, p. 105. Note the peculiar eighteenth-century usage, "goes down."

39. Mr. Singletary's scriptural burst was brought on by the patriotic appeal of Fisher Ames to "those who stood forth in 1775 to stand forth now" and vote for union. Singletary had served then but he had not contended with Great Britain "for a three penny tax on tea" as some said. "It was not that; it was because they claimed a right to tax us and bind us in all cases whatever. And does not this Constitution do the same?" *Ibid.*, II, p. 102.

As an "illiterate man" possibly Mr. Singletary did not know that his image of the Leviathan State had been used with telling effect by Hobbes, the great English absolutist of the Seventeenth Century. It is significant, too, that Parrington (*op. cit.*, I, p. 292 ff.) finds here the key to Alexander Hamilton's philosophy with its constant urge to advance the material power and splendor of the United States. Parrington also has pointed out that the authorities drawn on by the Federalists, before and after ratification, in the main were the older English theorists of the preceding century who were generally anti-democratic, and advocated the principle of coercive sovereignty whether by king or parliament. In this group there was no hint of the theory of the diminished state which Jefferson was later to embrace so eagerly. (Parrington, I, p. 280.)

40. Elliot, IV, p. 322. Pinckney was also careful to emphasize the advantages accruing to South Carolina from the abolition of paper money. "Experience has shown that in every state where it has been practiced . . . it always carries the gold and silver out of the country and impoverishes it." As a result it bears hard on foreign merchants and is ever "a discouragement to commerce." South Carolina "has productions useful to other countries and can always command a sufficient sum in specie to answer as a medium for the purposes of carrying on this commerce; provided there is no paper money." (p. 334.)

41. Elliot, IV, p. 20. *Cf.* MacLain, "I do not pretend to a great knowledge in trade, but I know something of it. If our trade be in a low situation, it must be the effect of our present weak government." (p. 189.)

Also the argument of Mr. Steele that without power to tax equally as they saw fit "the other powers of Congress would be nugatory." Though taxes might bear heavily for a little a long view showed it would give strength and respectability to the U. S. in times of war, "would promote industry and frugality, and would enable the Government to protect and extend commerce, and consequently increase the riches and population of the country." (p. 87.)

42. A speech of General Pinckney, of S. C. Elliot, IV, p. 286.

43. Elliot, IV, p. 102. Mr. Iredell speaking.

44. *Ibid.*, III, pp. 44-45. *Cf.* his later remark, "When power is given to this government . . . the language it assumes is clear, express, and unequivocal; but when this Constitution speaks of privileges, there is an ambiguity, sir, a fatal ambiguity. . . ." (p. 46.)

45. Elliot, IV, p. 202.

46. *Federalist,* IV. It is not to be thought that union is only to offer the benefits of defensive security. Jay and Hamilton both look to the time when a strong national government, through a navigation act and wise regulation of commerce, would call forth "all the national means and materials" for forming great fleets justly celebrated for their "prowess" and "thunder." In the meantime, Hamilton declares, although we can have no fleet equal to those of the great maritime powers we can create a navy of "respectable weight" ready to cast "into the scale of either of two contending parties." "A price

will be set not only upon our friendship, but upon our neutrality," for a few opportunely sent ships of the line "would often be sufficient to decide the fate of a campaign." We may hope to become "the arbiter of Europe in America" and be able to incline the balance of European *competitions* in this part of the world, as our interests may dictate. (*Federalist*, XI.) See also *Federalist*, VI, with its frank recognition of war as an accepted feature of national policy.

47. *Federalist*, IV.

48. *Federalist*, XI.

49. *Federalist*, XII.

50. *Federalist*, XI.

51. *Federalist*, VII. The passage continues, ". . . so that each particular State shall enjoy all sovereignty and supreme authority to all intents and purposes, excepting only those high authorities and powers by them delegated to Congress for the purposes of the general union."

52. Webster's pamphlet was published February, 1783. There is no mention of it by any delegate in either correspondence or during the debates. It probably did not receive wide circulation.

53. *Vd., infra*, p. 174 ff.

54. Some seven years later this paper and other materials were gathered together and published as *A View of the United States of America . . . between the years 1787 and 1794 . . . the whole tending to exhibit the progress and present state of civil and religious liberty, population, agriculture, exports, imports, fisheries, navigation, ship-building, manufactures, and general improvement.* London, 1795. First published Philadelphia, 1794. The original manuscript with its suggestions for the regulation of commerce are preserved in the text. A series of footnotes points out departures from the author's proposals in the actual provisions of the Constitution.

55. Tench Coxe's footnote here "As regular occupations" makes clear the distinction between the agricultural and commercial economy. *Ibid.*, p. 7.

56. *Ibid.*, pp. 11-12. In the later edition the author remarks in a footnote: "The plan of the Convention was not at that time known. Instead of a power to lay particular duties being granted to Congress the better grant of a power to regulate our national commerce was made."

57. *Ibid.*, p. 13. In a footnote, edition of 1794: "From the clause in the Federal Constitution which secures this advantage, a great spring is given to the coasting trade and to American manufactures."

58. Although his specific suggestions were not adopted, Tench Coxe was eminently satisfied with the result. In an *ex post facto* footnote he scribbles, "The power over commerce granted by the Federal Constitution is far preferable to this" and declares the clause to be "no less favorable to commerce than to private virtue and national honor." In an epilogue to the completed work he congratulates the nation upon "the measures of the Convention of 1787 . . . in the establishment of a national legislature with complete powers over commerce and navigation, defence, war and peace, money and all the other great objects of national economy." *Ibid.*, pp. 32-33.

59. It is often overlooked that in the regular course of their duties, administrative and legislative officers of the United States habitually interpret the Constitution.

60. *American State Papers*, Commerce and Navigation, VII, #9. Jefferson's forgotten report communicated to the House of Representatives, December 9, 1791, anticipates Marshall's famous doctrine of *Gibbons v. Ogden* by more than thirty years.

61. *American State Papers*, Class III, Finance, Vol. I, #31, p. 123 ff. Report on Manufactures made to Congress December 5, 1791. The actual authorship of the document is still in dispute. Hamilton thanks Tench Coxe for "literary help." Joseph Dorfman, who has studied the matter, is persuaded that the style and the march of argument reveal the workmanship of Coxe.

62. *Ibid.*, p. 123.

63. *Ibid.*, p. 135. William Graham Sumner came to the same conclusion in writing his life of Hamilton some forty years ago. Hamilton's system, he said, "is the old system of mercantilism of the English School turned around and adjusted to the situation of the United States." (*op. cit.*, p. 175.) There can be no question that Hamilton was in complete accord with all the traditional doctrines current in the late Eighteenth Century, including the balance of trade theory that the "introduction and circulation of precious metals, those darling objects of human avarice . . . serves to vivify and invigorate the channels of industry and to make them flow with greater activity and copiousness." (*Federalist*, XII.)

64. "Considering a monopoly of the domestic market to its own

manufactures as the reigning policy of manufacturing nations, a similar policy . . . is dictated, it might almost be said, by the principles of distributive justice. . . ."

65. In the New World, however, agriculture was of unusual importance, and therefore "the prohibition of the export of the materials of manufacture should be indulged in sparingly."

66. "From some views the best policy," as a tariff helps the manufacture only in the home market and has "no tendency . . . to promote . . . exportation."

67. "This is a point of considerable moment to trade in general, and to manufactures in particular, by rendering more easy the purchase of raw materials and provisions and the payment for manufactured supplies."

68. In fact, except for the lack of prohibitions upon the emigration of any skilled artisan and upon the exportation of any American invention, it is hard to think of mercantilists' policies which are not in Hamilton's list.

69. As mercantilism gave way to *laissez-faire* the general significance of Hamilton's *Report on Manufactures* was lost. A thread of mercantilism policy survived—but greatly transformed—in the doctrine of "the high tariff," and the Report came to be interpreted in terms of the nineteenth-century controversy between protection and free trade.

70. Speech of January 11, 1790. *Annals of Congress;* Richardson's *Messages of the President's,* I.

71. The first paragraph of the Randolph plan read:

"Resolved that the articles of Confederation ought to be so corrected and enlarged as to accomplish the objects proposed by their institution; namely, common defence, security of liberty and general welfare." Farrand, I, p. 20.

72. "A good law is that, which is . . . withall Perspicuous . . . The Perspicuity, consisteth not so much in the words of the Law it selfe, as in a Declaration of the Causes, and Motives, for which it was made. That is it, that shewes us the meaning of the Legislator; and the meaning of the Legislator known, the Law is more easily understood by few, than many words. For all words, are subject to ambiguity; and therefore multiplication of words in the body of the Law, is multiplication of ambiguity: Besides it seems to imply, (by

too much diligence,) that whosoever can evade the words, is without the compasse of the Law—Thomas Hobbes, *Leviathan,* 1651 (Everyman ed.), pp. 185-6.

73. It is the way, not of the lawyer, but of the legalist, to construe the document clause by clause as if each provision were an intellectual entity, and as if the meaning were to be drawn from the words themselves. Such an uncritical procedure opens the way for the unconscious intrusion of the ideas in the interpreter's head into the lines of the document. The wise expositor is aware that the details of injunctions and imperatives are but the henchmen of a large intent and looks to the purposive document as a whole for guidance. If the evidence of contemporary circumstance is to be accepted, such a procedure is compelled by the nature of the document.

74. It hardly needs to be set down—though it is often forgotten—that the Tenth Amendment, reserving to the States or to the People the powers not specifically granted, takes away nothing from the powers granted.

75. In terms of the elementary logic of law, the Constitution sets down only a major premise. The minor premise belongs always to the realm of contemporary fact. This is elementary, even obvious. Yet its implications are often overlooked. It limits, for instance, the use of precedents having to do with interstate commerce to instances in which there has been no substantial change in the activities in question.

76. It is often forgotten, even in constitutional interpretation, that it is not physical things but the conduct of individuals with which the law is concerned. Its domain is a society of activities and relationships. Where a thing categorically belongs cannot be determined in the abstract. Where goods physically move is inconsequential in itself; it is the activity to which their movement is related that matters. It all depends upon what question of law has been raised—and perhaps ultimately upon why one wants to know.

77. A study should be made, in the law reports and other records of public opinion, of the prestige and decline of the war power. In the later Eighteenth Century, when competitive nationalism was dominant, its comprehensive scope was hardly questioned. It was quite sufficient to justify the imposition of a scheme of regulation upon all activities that promoted the opulence of the commonwealth. In the Nineteenth Century, with its less turbulent struggle between

states and its greater concessions to *laissez-faire*, its scope was narrower and it was far less frequently invoked. The Great War of the second decade of the present century made it evident that wars are fought by industrial economies as well as by armies. It came after almost a century of a relative commitment to pacifism; and, instead of ending war, seems to have ushered in another period of competitive nationalism. Lagging concepts are slowly remade; and a redefinition of "the war power" in an industrial civilization still awaits judicial statement.

78. It is not without significance that American shipowners were granted a monopoly of the coastwise carrying trade.

79. The modern instruments of credit were not excluded from federal regulation; they have, with the change in our economy, usurped the dominant role of money. A genetic analysis of the credit economy is badly needed. A bank-bill ceases to be a receipt for money and comes to perform a function of its own. So new usages have little by little, without any clean-cut break, transformed old ways of finance. Alexander Hamilton, pushed by American circumstances, seems to have been among the pioneer thinkers who conceived of a bank as an instrument for the creation of credit. A recognition of this simple historical fact simplifies the over-elaborated questions raised in the gold-clause cases. *Vd., supra.*, p. 48.

80. There has been of late quite a bother over whether "the general welfare" as set down in Article I, Section 8, clause 1, is an objective of the spending power or is a separate and distinct grant of power to Congress. Such a question belongs to the first half of the Twentieth, not the last half of the Eighteenth, Century. The list of enumerated powers is an injunction to Congress to promote the general welfare—not a nebulous indefinable general welfare—but the general welfare as it was understood at the time. Hamilton in his *Report on Manufactures* states it thus:

"It is, therefore, of necessity, left to the discretion of the National Legislature to pronounce upon the objects which concern the general welfare, and for which, under that description, an appropriation of money is requisite and proper. And there seems to be no room for a doubt that whatever concerns the general interests of learning, of agriculture, of manufactures, and of commerce, are within the sphere of the national councils, as far as regards an application of money.

"The only qualification of the generality of the phrase in question which seems to be admissible, is this: That the object to which an appropriation of money is to be made be general, and not local; its operation extending in fact or by possibility throughout the Union, and not being confined to a particular spot.

"No objection ought to arise to this construction, from a supposition that it would imply a power to do whatever else should appear to Congress conducive to the general welfare. A power to appropriate money with this latitude, which is granted, too, in express terms, would not carry a power to do any other thing not authorized in the Constitution, either expressly or by fair implication." (loc. cit., at p. 136.)

81. Compare the argument recently developed by the United States Supreme Court that the power of Congress over "commerce among the several States" is more limited than our "foreign commerce." Professor Corwin (op. cit., pp. 23-52) devotes a chapter to this proposition in its various phases. It was advanced originally by Madison late in life but made no converts on the Supreme Bench until 1901. Then Justice Fuller, in a series of dissents, later continued by Justice White, revived the doctrine. It was finally accepted by a majority of the Court, in qualified form, in the first Child Labor Case. Hammer v. Dagenhart, 247 U.S. 251 (1918).

It is of note that in the AAA decision Justice Roberts felt called upon to exempt the "protective" tariff from his sweeping generalization by a footnote. That "tax," expropriating money "from one group for the benefit of another," and directly aimed at affecting the "local" business of manufacture within a State, is preserved because it rests on the Congressional power over foreign commerce.

CHAPTER VII

1. The most recent use of "direct" and "indirect" effects as criteria of congressional jurisdiction over interstate commerce is to be found in the Schechter and Carter decisions. The latter decision, in the words of Professor Corwin (op. cit., p. 205), revives "the doctrine or rather the formula, of the Sugar Trust Case, which classified as 'indirect' and hence outside the power of Congress . . . any effects which might reach commerce from conditions surrounding production, 'however inevitable and whatever the extent' of such effects."

2. In 1918 in Hammer v. Dagenhart, loc. cit., the Court had held void an act of Congress prohibiting interstate transportation of goods manufactured by child labor. Four years later it declared that a

special tax on the incomes of concerns employing such labor was invalid. *Bailey v. Drexal Furniture Co.*, 259 U.S. 20 (1922).

3. *U. S. v. Butler, loc. cit.*

4. The doctrine of states' rights, new style, must not be confused with the doctrine of states' rights, old style, which was touched off by the slave question and accorded a reputable place in Constitutional law. It is enough to remark that all the salients won by the older doctrine were lost in the period following the Civil War.

5. *Lochner v. New York*, 198 U.S. 45 (1905) at p. 75.

6. But, if the argument above has validity, the Constitution does embody an economic theory. It was this theory which Mr. Justice Holmes was trying to conserve—remade in a new age to the rather different necessity of social legislation.

7. A strange confusion prevails in the terms "liberal" and "conservative" as applied to members of the Supreme Court. As ordinarily used they are taken over from political discussion; they are certainly not indigenous to the intellectual usages of the Court. It is the so-called conservative majority who have read innovations into the law. It is the usefulness of the doctrines on which they stand to the "advancing cause of social legislation" which causes a certain group of justices to be looked on as liberals.

8. "Constitutional principles, applied as they are written, it must be assumed, operate justly and wisely as a general thing, and they may not be remolded by lawmakers or judges to save exceptional cases of inconvenience, hardship or injustice." Mr. Justice Sutherland, speaking for the majority in *Tyson v. Banton*, 273 U.S. 418 (1927).

9. In like manner the Supreme Court in making its decisions is "uninfluenced by predilection for or against the policy disclosed in legislation. The fact that . . . [a] scheme is novel is, of course, no evidence of [its] unconstitutionality. Even though we should consider the act unwise and prejudicial to both public and private interest, if it be fairly within delegated power our obligation is to sustain it. On the other hand though we should think the measure embodies a valuable social plan and be in entire sympathy with its purpose . . . if the provisions go beyond the boundaries of constitutional power we must so declare." Mr. Justice Roberts in *Railroad Retirement Board v. Alton.*

10. The courts have lately argued that necessity is no argument for

power; that federal authority cannot be spelled out from the incapacity of the states to regulate. But, where the matter is commerce, and already within the power of government, capacity might well serve as the principle of division of jurisdiction between nation and state.

Index

AAA, 12, 196, 244
Adams, Abigail, 58
agricultural interest, 71, 122-123,
160-161, 169, 170, 185. *See also*
landed interest
agriculture, 22, 72-73, 109, 113,
116, 120, 147, 167, 169, 176, 205,
213, 218, 224, 243; Coxe's view,
169-170; Franklin's eulogy to,
217-218; Jefferson's view on,
219; regulation of, 12, 196, 344;
status of in post-Revolutionary
America, 22, 169-170
Ames, Fisher, in Massachusetts
ratifying convention, 237
among, definition of, 232
Anderson, Adam, *An Historical
and Chronological Deduction
of the Origin of Commerce*,
198, 211
Annapolis Convention, 34-36, 169
Appalachian Coals Case, 197
art, definition of, 45 ff., 72
Articles of Confederation, 38
artisan, definition of, 47
*Ashwander v. Tennessee Valley
Authority*, 195

Bailey v. Drexal Furniture Co.,
245
balance of trade, doctrine of, 67,
83 ff., 170, 210, 220, 238
bank, definition of, 48
bank-bill, 48
bankrupt, 78-80, 215
bankruptcy, under the confederation, 30, 36; power to establish

uniform rules for, 118-119, 134,
181, 226
Beard, Charles A., *An Economic
Interpretation of the Constitu-
tion*, 202
*Bedford Cut-Stone Co. v. Jour-
neymen Stone-Cutters' Ass'n*,
197
Bedford, Gunning, delegate from
Delaware, 130; on the powers
of Congress, 129; on propor-
tional representation in the
Senate, 150, 152-153
Bellamy, Edward, *The Duke of
Stockbridge*, 199
Bill of Rights, 164
Blake, Edward, *King Edward
III*, 61
Board of Trade v. Olsen, 197
Bounties, 175
Bowdoin, James, in Massachusetts
ratifying convention, 161, 237
Brandeis, Associate Justice, U. S.
Supreme Court, 196, 197
Brimms, U. S. v., 197
Burke, Edmund, 209
Burney, Charles, *A General His-
tory of Music*, 211
business, definition of, 49 ff., 205
Butler, Associate Justice, U. S.
Supreme Court, 196, 197
Butler, Pierce, delegate from
South Carolina, on powers of
Congress, 128; on mercantilism,
146; on the sanctity of prop-
erty, 155
Butler, U. S. v., 195, 245